Former corporate lawyer, co-founder of a successful software company and technology investor, David Gillespie is the bestselling author of the *Sweet Poison* books, *Big Fat Lies*, *Free Schools*, *Toxic Oil*, *Eat Real Food*, *The Eat Real Food Cookbook*, *Teen Brain* and *The Good Fat Guide*. He lives in Brisbane with his wife and six children.

Also by David Gillespie

The *Sweet Poison* books
Big Fat Lies
Free Schools
Toxic Oil
Eat Real Food
The Eat Real Food Cookbook
Teen Brain
The Good Fat Guide

DAVID GILLESPIE

TAMING TOXIC PEOPLE

MACMILLAN

Pan Macmillan Australia

First published 2017 in Macmillan by Pan Macmillan Australia Pty Ltd
1 Market Street, Sydney, New South Wales, Australia, 2000

Reprinted 2017 (five times), 2018 (five times), 2019 (twice), 2020 (twice), 2021

Cataloguing-in-Publication entry is available
from the National Library of Australia
http://catalogue.nla.gov.au

Typeset in 11/18 pt by Midland Typesetters
Printed by IVE

To Lizzie, Frank, Tony and Beth, who all do the right thing – even when no-one is watching.

CONTENTS

INTRODUCTION

Imagine for a minute that you are carving your way, machete in hand, through impenetrable jungle in some terribly exotic place. You happen upon a clearing when suddenly you notice you are not alone. On the other edge of the glen, a stone's throw from you, stands a tiger. He is staring intently at you. Assessing you. He doesn't care whether you love your mother, what your favourite colour is or even that tomorrow is your birthday. To him, you are one of just three things: a meal, entertainment or too nasty to bother with.

The tiger will test you. He will growl, bare his teeth, or make an imperceptible, but swift, movement in your direction. These are all tests. He is probing you. Monitoring you for signs of strength or weakness. He will use every faculty millions of years of adaptation have given him, to determine whether you are trouble, or lunch.

You cannot reason with him, you cannot threaten him, you cannot plead for mercy. Your only chance of survival is to convince him that you are more trouble than you are worth. If you manage that, he will turn and walk away without a backward glance. If you can't, your goose is cooked. Well, eaten.

The tiger's cold assessment of your meal-worthiness is the same as the one your psychopathic boss, workmate, relative or lover performed on you within the first few seconds of meeting you. This is a book about convincing the tiger you are more trouble than you're worth. And if you are really brave, it is a book that can tell you how to catch and tame the tiger. After all, who wouldn't want a pet tiger?

I've had the misfortune to encounter a large number of psychopaths. No, I don't work in a psychiatric unit or a prison. I've run across these people in all manner of benign social and work settings. None of these people would satisfy a test for overt criminality. But many skate very close to the edge. Their skill is obtaining a benefit – using criminal or at least, immoral, means – without ever exposing themselves to the force of the law.

I've been thinking about writing an easy to understand guide to dealing with psychopaths for a long time. Over the years, I've spoken to hundreds of people about the ideas in this book. Every single one (and I mean Every. Single. One.) of those people, often complete strangers, knew exactly what I was talking about. Every single one of them had worked for, been related to, been taught by, been married to or been in a relationship with someone who they felt to be a psychopath. Every one of those people had been profoundly damaged by the experience and most wanted to share their stories as a warning to others and never speak of it again.

I didn't seek out people affected by psychopaths. These were just people I chatted to after giving book talks or interviews, or people I ran into at the coffee shop. The truly amazing thing is that once I described how I believed a psychopath behaved, not a single person could say they had never experienced it. Many did not know that they were describing a psychopath, but believe me, if you have been, or are, a psychopath's victim, you are not alone.

One common theme emerged from those conversations: confusion. Psychopaths confuse the hell out of us normal people. They behave in bizarre and often highly unpredictable ways. And as soon as we are entangled with them, we spend more time worrying about how to deal with them than we do running our own lives. A psychopath ties us in knots for months, years or even decades. And while they are doing that they are causing us emotional and, often, financial harm. Harm that we are unlikely to ever recover from.

This is the book I wish I'd had when I encountered my first (and my second and my third . . .) psychopath. In it I have dissected the evidence on what we know about these callous and parasitic humans. But, even more importantly, I have used that evidence to create a plan for dealing with them.

With this plan in hand you will recognise the difference between a psychopath and the rest of us (who I call empaths) and be able to spot them instantly. Once you know what you're dealing with you will be able to precisely predict how a psychopath will behave in any situation and use that knowledge to save yourself weeks, months and even years of emotional distress.

You will understand the science behind psychopathy and how it tells us YOU CAN NEVER CHANGE A PSYCHOPATH. So you won't waste your time and emotional energy trying.

You will also come to appreciate the role of empathy in human relations and how a psychopath's lack of empathy is the key to understanding why they are so dangerous.

You'll know why psychopaths gravitate towards certain industries and positions of power, and you'll understand that they usually get them because psychopathic traits are often very close to what we look for in leaders.

Critically, you will understand how we have changed our society to be the perfect breeding ground for psychopaths. Over the past two centuries we have systematically destroyed the collective instincts and societal rules which so successfully held them in check before. By gravitating towards a society where the desires of the individual trump community values, where communal property is non-existent and where profit is much more important than how it was achieved, we have created psychopath heaven.

But best of all, you will know with absolute certainty how to use this knowledge to manage a psychopath in common situations and how your behaviour can help us to psychopath-proof our society.

If you're ready to tame tigers rather than cower before them (and hope they go away), then read on.

What do psychopaths have to do with me (and you)?

I've always been a curious person. I was one of those irritating kids who always asked 'why?' and didn't stop asking until the answer made logical sense. When I was about ten, my dad signed up to one of those 'buy this encyclopedia in 1000 weekly instalments' deals for something called 'How it Works'. This was well before the internet, so it was the only practical way to give detailed answers to a kid as annoying as me. Every week, Dad would drop by the newsagent and pick up the latest instalment.

I've still got the ten-volume collection of hundreds of weekly instalments. And at the drop of a hat I could flip to how a jet engine works or how a telephone works or how the human heart works. That incessant need to know how things worked, or why they were the way they were, was a big part of why I started writing books. I didn't understand why sugar was poison, so I went looking for an answer. I didn't understand why manmade vegetable oils were toxic, so I went looking for an answer. And I didn't know how to deal with the poisonous and toxic people in my life or why they behaved the way they did, so I went looking for an answer. This is the book about what I found.

The thing I remember most from my first close encounter with a psychopath in business was my utter confusion. He seemed to continually do things that had the real potential to drive away our best workers. He was an odd mix of obsessive micromanager on some things and completely absent on other things. I've had many good managers in my various careers and they all shared one thing in common: once they were satisfied you knew what you were doing, they stayed out of your way. Those managers became a resource I could bounce ideas off but they rarely intervened in my day-to-day work. And even then only if I was clearly lost. The psychopath was very different. He was constantly meddling, making last-minute changes in direction, getting upset if I made a decision – any decision – and, in general, micromanaging the workplace. He implemented procedures which seemed to be aimed at monitoring what everybody was doing. He insisted that all decisions had to be made by him, no matter how small. There were enormous delays in getting even the smallest thing decided. And then sometimes, if it was a pet project of his, it would be fast-tracked past all possible hurdles. He trusted nobody and the impact on the business was devastating. Our once happy, harmonious and focused workplace started to fall apart. No one seemed to trust anyone else and there was continuous in-fighting. We all felt like we were being watched.

This manager also had an uncanny ability to convince those higher up than him that someone else was to blame. They were clearly impressed by him no matter what happened. Somehow he always managed to deflect blame to others. Often this would result in those people being fired or leaving. Our staff turnover went through the roof. Worse, the replacements he hired seem to be chosen based on how nice they were to him not how good they were at the job. But he didn't seem to care. While he was obsessive about the work practices of those beneath him, he never applied the same detailed eye to his decisions. They were always made on impulse, on the spot and with no input from anybody else. He was always late for meetings, always accepted credit and deflected blame, and always insisted on special treatment. For example, he always flew first class even though the company policy was economy.

He also played favourites, allowing some people little privileges in return for their loyalty. These people would often be deployed as his proxy in meetings. They could not make any decisions but they would convey his directives – 'No, we cannot go that way, the boss is against that.' Often the psychopath would be sitting in his office just down the hall and there was no good reason he couldn't be there himself, but his absence made it much harder to challenge his views. Sometimes, particularly obstinate employees would demand that the minion race off and seek the boss's opinion on an alternative approach. The minion would dutifully return with nothing changed.

This boss made a habit of giving select people subtle but excruciating public punishment. Everything the chosen victim said or did in a meeting would be challenged. Then, after the meeting, they would get the silent treatment. He would assign them a task and make it impossible for them to get the information or resources they needed, then he would make fun of their failure to perform at the next meeting. This could go on for weeks at a time and then suddenly it would switch to a new victim. Everyone kept their heads down, in case he decided to pick on them next.

There seemed to be no rhyme or reason as to who he favoured with rewards and who he didn't. And trying to figure out his motivations did my head in. His constant pitting of employees against each other significantly accelerated the destruction of trust in the workplace. Everyone was in it for themselves. No one knew who they could trust and, as a result, nobody trusted anyone. He often told me negative things about other employees. They were easy to believe because elements of things he said were true. Now, looking back, I realise I was just being used like the gullible fool I was. He was almost certainly doing the same thing with everyone else. He seemed to genuinely enjoy an environment where nobody trusted anyone else.

These were not the only things he lied about. The longer I knew him the more convinced I became that everything he said was a lie. Things that he told me years before did not gel with things he was telling me now. At first, I dismissed this as my inaccurate memory, and because I no longer trusted anyone at work there was no one to check with. So I started taking notes. It was then that his lies became obvious. They were rarely big lies but they were consistent and they always had a built-in level of deniability – meaning he always had wiggle room. If challenged on something he had said or done, he seemed to have a rational alternative explanation. Pinning him down was like pinning jelly to a wall.

In a state of total confusion and despair, I eventually turned to Google for answers. Surprisingly I found them very quickly. My boss's behaviour was an exact match to what bloggers and many scientists called a 'corporate psychopath'. They all used slightly different terms. Some called it 'psychopathy'. Some called it 'sociopathy'. Some went with 'narcissist'. And others just went with garden-variety 'micromanagers' and 'bullies'. But they were all describing the same type of personality that was sucking the life out of my job.

I realise now, with the benefit of hindsight, that my boss didn't care how good or bad my work was and didn't have the skills to tell anyway. But at the time, I felt I was constantly being judged and watched. I became paranoid and fearful, and worked even harder to complete impossible and pointless tasks within the ridiculous timeframes he was setting. I could have given him anything and spent my time looking for a new job instead. I wish I had known that at the time. It would have made a big difference. I would still have despaired at the pointlessness of it all but at least I wouldn't have taken it personally.

I also realised that I had come across these same patterns of behaviour in other people, in workplaces and in my personal life. The details differed but the modus operandi was always the same.

It didn't matter if they were female or male, old or young. It always boiled down to the same basic patterns of manipulation through divide and conquer. I had put these other people's micromanagement and manipulation down to personality quirks. But once I found the label for my boss's behaviour, I knew I was dealing with a very specific and dangerous personality type.

If this all sounds familiar to you, then you are not alone. I have discovered that almost everyone has a story like mine about someone they work with, are related to or are in a relationship with. People like my first psychopath are a part of everyone's lives every day. The purpose of this book is to provide guidance, not titillation. I want you to see how common psychopathic behaviour is and I want to give you the tools to deal with it. To that end, throughout the rest of the book, I've included examples from my own encounters and stories that people have told me about their interactions with psychopaths. Obviously all the names and many of the identifying circumstances have been changed to protect . . . well, to stop me being sued.

PART 1

THE
THEORY

1

A SHORT HISTORY OF PSYCHOPATHY

Psychopaths have been with us for as long as there has been an 'us', but we've taken a long time to nail down an agreed definition – and we're still not all on the same page. In this chapter I look at what we know about the condition, starting with psychological theories and progressing through to what the latest imaging technology is telling us about how psychopaths' brains are different.

What is a psychopath?

The word psychopath has almost as many different meanings as there are people writing about the person it describes. If you are a criminologist it means people who are just as likely to chop off your hand as shake it (and who feel roughly the same way about both options as long as there is a benefit to them). If you are a psychiatrist the word is meaningless because it isn't defined in the Diagnostic and Statistical Manual of Mental Disorders (DSM), the book of acceptable psychiatric diagnosis. If you are a human resources manager it means micromanagers and workplace bullies. If you are a psychologist it probably means someone who is a little bit worse than a sociopath, who in turn is a little bit worse than a narcissist. (And to make matters worse, the definitions of both of those terms are more than a little fluffy themselves.) To everybody else it means any, or all, of those things, but it is definitely not a compliment. Largely thanks to Hollywood, to most of us now a psychopath is a violent serial killer. And while some of them probably are, there is a much more dangerous version that we are more likely to encounter every day.

The word psychopath means literally 'diseased mind'. The 'psycho' bit comes from the Greek 'psyche', meaning 'mind', 'spirit' or 'soul'. The 'path' bit (also Greek, from 'pathos') means 'suffering' or 'disease'. When the word was invented by nine-teenth-century German psychiatrists, that's all it meant. It had the same meaning as when we now say a person is 'mentally ill'. In late nineteenth-century America, the term was used even more gener-ally. A 'psychopathic practitioner' was what we would now call a psychiatrist and their hospitals were referred to as 'psychopathic institutions'.

But by the turn of the twentieth century, the term was increas-ingly being used to describe anyone with a 'personality disorder' (or 'moral insanity' as it was then called) of any sort.

Personality disordered people account for between forty to sixty percent of all diagnosed mental disorders. These people behave in a way that doesn't fit in with society's expectations for social interaction. We all experience these behavioural disorders to some degree, but to score a diagnosis, they have to significantly and persistently impair our ability to function socially or occupationally.

These disorders are roughly divided into three groups but they are not mutually exclusive and many people are diagnosed as having more than one. The disorders are:

- **Odd disorders** (often associated with schizophrenia)
  Paranoid – irrational suspicion and mistrust
  Schizoid – detached from social relationships
  Schizotypal – extreme discomfort with social interaction

- **Dramatic disorders**
  Antisocial – disregard for others, lack of empathy and manipulative behaviour
  Borderline – instability in self-image, behaviour and relationships
  Histrionic – attention-seeking behaviour
  Narcissistic – need for admiration and a lack of empathy

- **Anxious disorders**
  Avoidant – feelings of inadequacy and extreme sensitivity
  Dependent – need for care from other people
  Obsessive-compulsive – rigid conformity to rules and perfectionism.

Up until the 1930s, describing someone as a psychopath meant they were broadly socially undesirable. They made a habit of breaking the law or moral and social conventions. The description was frequently used to distinguish 'moral insanity' from the more stigmatised 'lunacy' or 'insanity' that could get you locked up for a long time.

During the 1930s, courts and law-makers began using the term to describe sexual offenders, including, at that time, being homo-sexual. 'Sexual psychopaths' could be imprisoned indefinitely in many US states at the time and that use of the term probably didn't help to keep the word 'psychopath' on the pile of positive adjectives one could use about one's father-in-law. By World War II, psychologists, despairing at the multiple meanings for psycho-pathy (from a general personality disorder all the way through to a serial killer), coined the word 'sociopath'. The meaning of sociopath was essentially the same as the early twentieth-century meaning of psychopath. A sociopath was someone who had a personality disorder, but wasn't insane or a serial sex offender. The new word was an attempt to remove the judgemental aspects of the word 'psychopath' which were by then developing.

'KULANGETA': THE INUIT WORD FOR PSYCHOPATH?

Modern English speakers may not have settled on the correct word for it, but every group of humans has tended to include a word in their language that means a person who does their own thing with no regard for others.

The traditional Inuit of north-west Canada call them 'kulangeta'. They say that a kulangeta will repeatedly lie, cheat and steal; he won't go hunting for polar bear and, when the other men do, he takes advantage of their women. A kulangeta ignores reprimands and consequences despite repeated punishment. And if he can't be controlled, killing him is often the only option.

The first diagnoses

By the time the first edition of the diagnostic bible for American psychiatrists, the DSM, rolled out in 1952, the term 'sociopath' had become a lot more specific. From then on you could officially be diagnosed as having a 'Sociopathic Personality Disturbance'. One of the four subtypes of this 'disturbance' was 'antisocial', something the psychiatrist who suggested the classification called 'psychopathic'.

That psychiatrist was a chap by the name of Hervey M. Cleckley, who was the author of the first popular book on psychopathy, *The Mask of Sanity*. The book focused on a personality type which fascinated the American public and it was a massive bestseller. Cleckley's 'psychopath' was a master deceiver. He could pass a psychiatric test, but privately was a highly destructive personality. He knew no moral or ethical boundaries but appeared to function as a perfectly normal member of society. Cleckley believed that psychopaths were fundamentally incurable because their illness was an inborn unwillingness or inability to understand the moral and ethical rules by which society works. Notwithstanding this fundamental illness, they appeared normal, hence 'the mask of sanity'.

Cleckley referred to these types of people as psychopaths when the book was first published in 1941 but by the time the first edition of the DSM rolled off the presses eleven years later, the American public (following the lead of the psychiatric profession) was more likely to refer to them as sociopaths. It was the same thing but without the criminal overtones. By the time Alfred Hitchcock got into the act, with his 1960 movie, *Psycho*, the general public's definition of a psychopath was the type of bloke who chopped you up in the shower rather than your bullying boss or your highly manipulative girlfriend (see 'Psychopaths on screen' on page 44 for more on psychopaths in film).

But this didn't stop Cleckley continuing to describe antisocial sociopaths as psychopaths, and even expanding that definition over the decades to apply to people who were neither criminals nor prisoners.

The Hare Psychopathy Checklist

The second edition of the DSM came out in 1968 but still didn't include any diagnosis of psychopathy. Dr Robert Hare, a Canadian clinical psychologist who worked in prisons, developed a now famous checklist for identifying a psychopath based on Cleckley's criteria and his own observations in prison populations. The first version of Hare's checklist was released in 1980. The third edition of the DSM was coincidentally released in the same year. It redefined sociopaths as people with Antisocial Personality Disorder (but still gave no definition of 'psychopaths'). Hare has published many versions of his PCL (Psychopathy Check List) over the last three decades but they are all based on the traits first identified by Cleckley. Hare's PCLs are now widely used in the courts to determine the risk of a person re-offending and the probability of rehabilitation. People who score high on the PCL are theoretically unlikely to change their ways (although this is still highly controversial).

The checklist is made up of twenty personality traits divided into four groups called facets (interpersonal, affective, lifestyle and antisocial). The groups measure traits such as superficial charm, propensity to lie, lack of remorse, and a need for stimulation. Each of these twenty traits is scored (after a face-to-face interview and review of records) as a 0 (not present), 1 (present but not dominant) or 2 (dominant). The maximum score is obviously 40. The average person scores between 3 and 6. Non-psychopathic criminals score between 16 and 22. A total score of 30 or over in the United States (or 25 or over in the United Kingdom) is regarded as a positive diagnosis of psychopathy. Just to give us a sense of how these criteria might be applied, I've used my non-existent training in psychology to score James Bond.

CASE STUDY: JAMES BOND

PCL-R	James Bond
Facet 1: Interpersonal	
• Glibness or superficial charm	2 – Is it possible to be more charming than James Bond?
• Grandiose sense of self-worth	2 – A 'secret' agent who uses his own name all the time? Yup.
• Pathological lying	2 – Aside from his name, he does seem to lie an awful lot.
• Cunning or manipulative	2 – Obviously part of the job.
Facet 2: Affective	
• Lack of remorse or guilt	2 – James has killed over 350 people on screen so far and it never seems to trouble him in the slightest.

- Emotionally shallow

    2 – I'm sure he really does love all those women he sleeps with.

- Callous or lack of empathy

    2 – Has he ever seemed to experience another person's emotions? There was that one time when he cried in the shower with Vesper Lynd . . .

- Failure to accept responsibility for their own actions

    1 – Every now and then he does take the blame for stuffing up.

Facet 3: Lifestyle

- Need for stimulation (easily bored)

    2 – We never see him sitting around much, do we?

- Parasitic lifestyle

    2 – Everything seems to be on the expense account.

- Lack of realistic, long-term goals

    2 – Does he have any long-term goals?

- Impulsivity

    2 – He certainly struggles to contain his impulses when it comes to killing (and seducing) women.

- Irresponsibility

    1 – Occasionally he does things for king and country.

Facet 4: Antisocial

- Poor behavioural controls

    0 – He is in control most of the time.

- Early behavioural problems

    0 – We don't know so let's go with 0.

- Juvenile delinquency

    0 – Once again, we don't know.

• A history having conditional release from prison revoked	0 – We don't know.
• Criminal versatility	0 – His crimes are sanctioned by his 00 status.
Other Items	
• Many short-term marital relationships	1 – He's never been married but he has had many relationships that might have ended that way (had the other half not been killed off).
• Promiscuous sexual behaviour	2 – Is it possible to give more than 2?
Total	**27**

People who score highly in Facets 3 and 4 are more likely to be found on the wrong side of a prison wall. People who score highly on Facets 1 and 2 are more likely to be your boss, your partner, a family member or, apparently, a secret agent. James managed a score that makes him a psychopath in the UK but not quite one in the US. The unflappable, focused, but erudite and charming killer that Bond represents is not a million miles from the kind of person this book is about.

Psychopathy or antisocial personality disorder?

The official psychiatric diagnosis equivalent to psychopathy is antisocial personality disorder (ASPD). The DSM description of ASPD is long-winded and opaque but luckily the Mayo Clinic has provided this handy summary. ASPD is:

'a mental condition in which a person consistently shows no regard for right and wrong and ignores the rights and feelings of others. People with antisocial personality disorder tend to antagonize, manipulate or treat others harshly or with callous indifference. They show no guilt or remorse for their behavior.'

Hare maintains that this is not detailed enough. He says that eighty-five percent of criminals would easily meet the ASPD criteria but only twenty percent of those are genuine psychopaths. More importantly, he says that those twenty percent are responsible for half of all serious crime. Psychopaths are generally regarded by psychologists as beyond cure and are four to eight times as likely to re-offend as non-psychopaths. If the point of diagnosis is to identify dangerous psychopaths then using a test which almost every criminal satisfies is not particularly helpful.

Despite there still being no official diagnosis of psychopathy in the DSM, there is little doubt psychopaths are not what most of us would describe as mentally 'normal'. But they are also not what we think of when we think of the mentally ill. They don't suffer from hallucinations. They aren't anxious or compulsive. They don't hear voices. They aren't socially awkward. But they are sometimes guilty of the most outrageously violent crimes and show absolutely no remorse for their victims.

Obviously, a big problem with the official diagnosis and Hare's PCL is that both are an attempt to diagnose a condition which is based on convincingly lying about who and what you are. Paradoxically, the higher a person would really score on the first two facets (which include charm, lying and a lack of guilt), the less likely you are to be able to tell by talking to them. Hare's test might be just dandy for deciding if the serial killer seeking parole is likely to keep killing but it's likely to be of little use in identifying the kinds of psychopaths most of us should be interested in.

To identify and deal with those people, we need to use significantly more sophisticated tools than a checklist and a criminal history check.

THE FUNERAL TEST

There is an internet meme that says you can detect a psychopath by getting them to answer just one question. Here's how one popular version goes:

This is a genuine psychological test. It is a story about a girl.

While at the funeral of her mother, she met a guy she did not know.

She thought he was amazing – her dream guy – and she fell in love with him there and then . . . A few days later, the girl killed her sister.

Question: What is her motive in killing her sister?

DON'T scroll down until you have thought what your answer is to this question!

Answer: She was hoping that the guy would appear again at the next family funeral.

If you answered this correctly, you think like a psychopath. This test was designed by a famous American psychologist to see if you have the same mentality as a killer. Many arrested serial killers took part in this test and answered it correctly. If you didn't answer correctly – good for you. If your friends hit the jackpot, may I suggest that you keep your distance. (If you got the answer correct, please let me know so I can take you off my distribution list . . .)

This is, of course, nonsense. Psychopaths do not perceive the world in terms of 'Who can I kill to get what I want?' Most of them would struggle as much as anyone else to give the correct answer. Curiously, the only person I know who got it right first time was my mother-in-law – hmmm . . .

In an ironic twist, however, something very close to this scenario played out in the news. In October 2016, Samuel Velasco Gurrola from El Paso, Texas, was found guilty of murdering his wife at her sister's funeral – after he killed both her sister and father to lure her there. He wanted to kill his estranged wife before she testified against him in a sexual assault case, so he hired a hitman to murder his wife's father. The idea being that she would be lured to the funeral where he could kill her. That didn't work out, so he had her sister killed. This time the wife was murdered by the hitman at the funeral. The sexual assault case was dismissed as the main witness was dead.

What motivates a psychopath?

Now that we know what a psychopath is, the obvious question is why. Why are they the way they are? It is a question that has been the focus of sustained research for decades.

Psychologists have always firmly believed that psychopaths are wired differently to the rest of us. As early as 1964, researchers noted that psychopathic criminals had an exaggerated craving for excitement when compared to similar, but non-psychopathic, criminals. The psychopathic criminals were more likely to want to do risky things. The things that provided a 'buzz'. Things like having multiple sexual partners (often at the same time but without the others knowing), drinking and gambling. They were also more likely to try and use a greater range of drugs. Psychopaths received greater rewards (or a bigger 'hit') than empaths from the same rewarding activity. Simultaneously, the research I'm about to explain shows they also don't fear negative consequences anywhere near as much as empaths.

EMPATHS

I regard the world as being divided into two types of people: empaths and psychopaths. Empath is a word from the paranormal world. It means someone who has a paranormal ability to perceive the emotional state of another person. Compared to psychopaths, I reckon we're all empaths. From now on I'll use it to describe us normal folk. It sounds so much less clinical than the more politically correct 'neurotypical'. An empath sounds like someone you'd like to be around; a neurotypical, not so much.

Psychopaths and fear conditioning

Humans and animals can be trained. Psychologists call this 'conditioning'. In 1901 Ivan Pavlov showed that a dog's salivation reflex could be trained by sounding a bell just before food was presented. The dogs would then salivate when the bell rang even if there was no food. In 1920, psychologist Dr John Watson from Johns Hopkins University showed this also worked in humans, or more specifically a single baby human, dubbed Little Albert. Watson and his graduate student Rosalie Rayner set out to demonstrate that a human could easily be trained to fear something that was not inherently frightening. Some of our responses are hardwired by evolution. For example, we fear snakes because people who fear snakes tended to live to reproduce and so the fear became a favourable adaptation. There is, however, no evolutionary mechanism to provide us with a hardwired fear of stoves.

Watson and Rayner chose a nine-month-old infant, who they called Albert B. For the first part of the experiment they allowed him to play with a white laboratory rat. Albert had never seen the small furry animal before and happily touched and played with it. They also showed him other things such as burning paper, a dog, a monkey and several masks that looked like furry animals. He was not afraid of any of them.

In the next phase of the experiment, Albert was again allowed to play with the rat but every time he touched it a very loud sound would be made behind him. Albert responded to the noise the way any nine month old would. He got very upset. The rat and noise scenario was performed several more times. After that, Albert just had to see the rat and he would cry and try to crawl away. He had been conditioned very quickly to fear something that he did not fear at all before.

Shortly after conducting the experiment, Dr Watson was dismissed from Johns Hopkins for having an affair with Ms Rayner. Psychologists were naturally interested to know whether there were any long-lasting effects on Albert but Watson refused to tell anyone who Albert B was. The hunt took the better part of a century but, in 2014, researchers published the results of decades of sleuthing.

Albert B was Albert Barger, the son of sixteen-year-old Pearl Barger, a wet nurse at the hospital on the Johns Hopkins

University campus. Pearl had died in 1939 and Albert in 2007, but the researchers were able to track down Albert's niece, Dorothy Parthree, in 2010. Dorothy remembered that Albert did indeed have a lifelong aversion to dogs and to furry animals in general. He was not pathological about it but she remembered having to put the family dog in another room whenever he visited. She also recalled that when he heard dogs barking he would instinctively clasp his hands over his ears.

In one short experiment done when Albert was just nine months old, he had potentially been programmed with a fear that stayed with him his entire life. Don't let anyone ever tell you that emotions, or at least fear, cannot be programmed.

In the late 1970s and early 1980s fear conditioning was used in a series of studies (once again performed on criminals) to demonstrate that psychopaths do not feel fear in the same way as empaths – or at least that it doesn't affect their behaviour. Those studies used a count-up to a painfully loud noise of 120 decibels – about the same as standing next to the speakers at a heavy metal rock concert. Based on the Little Albert experiment (and many like it since then), the psychologists knew that humans quickly learned to fear the impending sound. All the subjects knew what was coming, but as the count increased the psychopaths remained calm in the face of a known punishment while the normal people freaked out (that is, of course, the scientific term – they became noticeably stressed). Researchers were certain the psychopaths felt the punishment as much as the empaths. They were not supermen. It's just that the prospect of punishment did not worry them as much as it did the empaths. Psychopaths could not be fear-conditioned the way Little Albert had been.

The psychopath's desire for reward

Further studies in the 1990s experimented with using a reward as well as a punishment. Those studies found that when the experiment involved both punishment and reward, the psychopaths' responses showed they got a huge buzz from winning but losing barely affected them. Non-psychopaths were the opposite. Losing affected them much more than winning.

This type of study usually involves a game with real money at stake. Participants are first tested for psychopathic traits and then the results for psychopaths are compared to those for empaths. In the first type of study, subjects are shown two-digit numbers in random order. Some of the numbers are 'good' numbers and some are 'bad'. Good numbers result in a small monetary reward if the subject presses a button when the number is shown. If the button is pressed when a bad number is shown, the subject loses money. By trial and error, the subject needs to work out which numbers are good and which are bad and follow a strategy that maximises the amount of money they get to keep.

There are two types of error the subject can make. They can fail to press the button when a good number appears. This does not result in a fine and is called an error of omission – failing to do something that could have got them a reward. The other error is to press the button when a bad number appears. This will earn them a fine and is called an error of commission. Multiple studies on very divergent populations have shown that a psychopathic person makes many more errors of commission – pressing the button on a bad number – than a normal person. They are chasing the reward with little regard to the risk of the fine. They don't, however, make any more omission errors – failing to press when a good number appears – than empaths. Psychopaths and empaths both fail to pick the good numbers at the same rate. It's just that the psychopaths rush in where empaths fear to tread when there is a reward at stake. They are risk-takers if a reward is in play.

A shorthand way of saying this is losing hurts. But it does not affect a psychopath as much as an empath. And winning is good for empaths, but it's fantastic (and well and truly worth the potential loss) if you're a psychopath. This behaviour is the exact opposite of people with depression. Depressives exaggerate the negative and minimize the positive. Depression is characterised by social withdrawal and strong avoidance tendencies. A psychopath is characterised by excessive social approach behaviour (charm) in pursuing someone or something they desire and very low avoidance behaviour (low anxiety).

Psychopaths are therefore much less inhibited than the rest of us. This is what the psychologists call a strong 'behavioural activation system'. And psychopaths are much less concerned about punishment than the rest of us (a weak 'behavioural inhibition system'). In an empath, the activation system is in balance with the inhibition system and needs to be pushed in one direction or another before we take action. In a psychopath, the activation system is dominant and pushes them towards impulsive action. In depressives, the inhibition system is dominant and pushes them towards inaction. A psychopath is as capable of becoming depressed as I am of giving birth to triplets.

In practice this means empaths would worry about rejection, psychopaths wouldn't. They don't need a few rums to temporarily disable their inhibitions and embolden their approach to the hot girl in the bar. It's probably a salient warning to young ladies hanging out in bars. If the charming bloke who confidently approached you is drinking soda water, be cautious, he may be a psychopath – or he could just be on a sugar-free diet and be very keen on you.

The studies also show that when psychopaths are presented with more complex reward and punishment tasks their impulsivity and attitude to risk becomes even more visible. These studies often present random patterns on a screen for a limited amount of time. The subject is asked to decide if the patterns match or not by pressing one of two buttons. If they get it right they get a monetary reward and if they get it wrong they lose money. Empaths' responses slow down if they get one wrong. They tend to think about things more in an attempt to get the next one right. But psychopaths speed up! It's as if they are even more motivated to get the next reward and are not concerned that they were punished or that they might be punished again. They don't seriously contemplate the possibility they could be wrong or, if they do, it doesn't change their behaviour. The punishment has no aversive effect on them at all. The negative feedback doesn't impact on their self-belief. Empaths might consider the possibility that their strategy was wrong, but, having succeeded with a strategy before, the psychopath is convinced that they are infallible and will not let details (like losing) mess with that perception.

When similar studies measure stress indicators like heart rates and skin conduction in response to those rewards and punishment, they find psychopaths respond physically more than the empaths to both punishment and reward. They know they are being punished but the effect is the opposite to an empath. If anything, it makes the psychopaths more determined to get the reward next time. In real life, this looks like the boss who makes snap decisions based on zero research: 'Let's open an office in Singapore! The market there is exploding. Sure, we have never opened a second office before, and we know nothing about the Singapore market, but it's worth the risk because the rewards could be fantastic if it comes off.'

THE WISCONSIN CARD SORT TEST

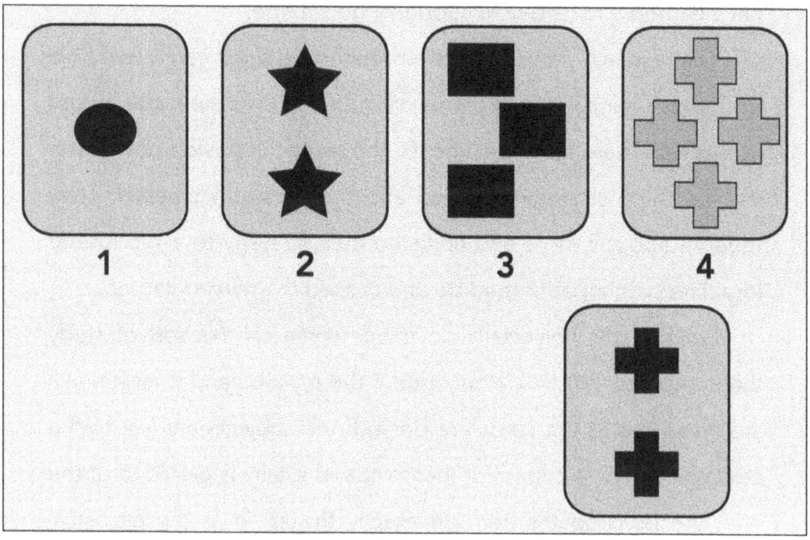

Figure 1: The Wisconsin Card Sort Test

More complex studies show that when it comes to adjusting strategy in response to negative feedback, the psychopath's hunger for reward can be a significant impairment. This type of study shows subjects cards one by one. They are told to match the cards they are given but not told the correct rule for matching. In the pictured example, the rule might be match colours (you can't see it but each card is a different colour), in which case card 1 would be correct; or it could be to match the number of shapes so card 2 would be correct; or it might be to match the shape, so card 4 would be correct. If the subject starts putting the cards in the right piles according to the undisclosed rule, they get a monetary reward for each correct card. If they are wrong, they are fined. By trial and error, the subjects quickly figure out how to sort the cards for maximum reward. At this point the researchers change the rule for matching cards without telling the subjects other than through the reward and punishment feedback. A card that previously would have earned a reward now suddenly gets a fine.

The research shows that psychopaths are significantly less able to change their previously chosen strategy, even as the losses mount up. As with the other experiments, the empaths slowed down after the matching strategy changed and their losses increased. They thought about it more and adjusted their strategy to avoid further loss. The psychopaths sped up and chased the reward harder.

Psychopaths universally do much worse on this sort of study than empaths. But this is only true if the rewards and punishments are given out as the cards are dealt. If the subjects are just told a card placement is correct or incorrect and a tally is provided at the end, the psychopaths perform exactly the same as the empaths. As long as the psychopath's desire for reward remains actively in play, they cannot easily change strategy. But if it is theoretical, they don't do any better or worse than the rest of us. The presence of palpable reward seems to produce an 'action stations' response in psychopaths. When they are in this state, they are hyper-alert and ready to respond quickly. They are also highly resistant to changing their planned response. Instant gratification has the same effect on psychopaths as a rum or ten has on the rest of us: it disables their inhibitions and makes them want to chase the reward harder. Needless to say, the consequences are pretty similar too, when it comes to the decisions they make about successful strategies. It might be good to bear that in mind if you want to put a psychopath in charge of your business (or country). They will do about as well as someone who is drunk most of the time – perhaps without the stumbling. Every now and then the risky call will pay off, but mostly it will be a disaster because nothing has been carefully researched and planned.

A (nearly) complete model of the psychopathic mind

By the end of the twentieth century, psychologists thought they had a pretty good model of psychopathy based on experiments like those described above. The exaggeration of reward and the minimisation of punishment explained a lot of what had been observed about their behaviour over the preceding century:

- Psychopaths are **charming** because they focus on what they can get from the person they are talking to rather than the possibility of rejection.
- They are **impulsive** because rewards loom larger than punishments and so they see little point in delaying gratification.
- They need **stimulation** (are easily bored) because the 'need for speed' is great – they get a significantly greater reward from risk than the rest of us do.
- They have a **grandiose sense of self-worth** because they don't remember negative experiences (like the ninety-nine girls who threw a drink in their face or the fine they just got for pressing the wrong button) but they do remember positive experiences (like the one girl who said yes).

This paints a picture of the psychopath as an impulsive, focused, reward-chasing, risk-ignoring go-getter. Throw the occasional bit of good luck into that mix and they could get some very big wins in business. A lucky psychopath can look good, at least until the next impulsive roll of the dice.

The reward and punishment theory can't, however, provide a complete explanation for the single biggest defining psychopathic trait: their total **lack of empathy**. Tantalisingly, there have been clues that there are underlying physical differences linking the psychopath's cyborg-like lack of fear and their lack of emotional experience in general and empathy in particular (see Chapter 2 for more about this).

My definition of a psychopath

Take another look at the psychopathy checklist on page 19. I reckon just about every teenager in an individualistic society like ours would score pretty well on all of Facet 3 (easily bored, parasitic lifestyle, lack of realistic long-term goals, impulsivity and irresponsibility) and the first item of Facet 4 (poor behavioural controls). And just about everyone with an Instagram account scores off the chart for most of Facet 1 (superficial charm, grandiose sense of self-worth, pathological lying, and cunning or manipulative). This doesn't mean your average selfish teen on Insta is a psychopath. It just means they're a teenager.

In my experience with real-life psychopaths, Facet 2 (lack of remorse or guilt, emotionally shallow, callous or lack of empathy, and failure to accept responsibility for their own actions) is the quintessential component. In individualistic societies, like the US, Australia or the UK, where everyone is behaving like a grandiose self-centred twat, it is not helpful to tell people to be on the lookout for grandiose self-centred twats. No, the defining difference of psychopaths is empathy, or, rather, the lack of it.

THE DIFFERENCE BETWEEN FEELINGS AND EMOTIONS

Emotions are gut reactions. They are primitive responses to situations which are hardwired into our pre-human brain. We experience emotions automatically and there aren't many. One popular psychological description says we have eight: Fear, Anger, Sadness, Joy, Disgust, Surprise, Trust and Expectation, but there is no definitive list.

Emotions can be measured. When we experience an emotion all kinds of uncontrollable changes to blood pressure, skin conductance, heart rate and expressions occur. Emotions are intense, powerful and short-lived. They are connected to our biochemistry. Without them, we would not know to run from a tiger, or seek out pleasure.

Feelings are the higher order thought models we create based on emotions. Feelings are processed in our frontal cortex. They are our automated, higher-order reactions to emotions and each of us develops these as we grow. They are a consequence of the human brain controlling and managing raw emotions.

We have hundreds of feelings but very few underlying emotions. Feelings are much less intense than emotions but last much, much longer.

Physical desire is an emotion but love is a feeling.

Fear is an emotion but anxiety is a feeling.

Psychopaths experience emotions but do not experience feelings. Their emotional state does not drive an automatic behavioural consequence.

Every free-range psychopath I have encountered or heard about has, at their core, a complete and total lack of empathy. They understand feelings as much as I understand quantum physics (so, not at all). That lack of empathy drives emotional shallowness – it's hard to have feelings about others if you don't understand how people around you feel. I imagine asking a psychopath to describe a feeling is like asking a blind person to describe a colour they have never seen. They probably know the name but nothing else about it. It's my belief that lack of empathy accounts for their lack of remorse and inability to accept responsibility. If I don't care how you feel about something, why should I feel sorry for how my actions affect you?

You don't feel sorry for the grass you mow on a Saturday afternoon and, to the best of my estimation, that's probably how a psychopath feels about people they harm. This is not to say that the other facets in the PCL are not frequently parts of a psychopath's character, but I don't believe they are as critical. You can have inflated self-worth and not be a psychopath. You can be manipulative and not be a psychopath. You can be a chronic liar and not be a psychopath. But in my opinion, if you lack empathy you are a psychopath whether you possess any of the other facets or not.

This is my definition of a psychopath. It is not the same as how Hare defines them. It is not the same (although not a long way from) the way Cleckley defined them. And it is definitely not the way a psychiatrist who follows the DSM would define them – largely because there is still not an official condition called psychopathy. But it is probably pretty close to what most of us think of when we hear the words 'sociopath' or 'malignant narcissist' or any of the other words that are supposed to be less offensive than calling someone a psychopath.

When I describe someone as a psychopath it is really just a shorthand way of saying a person who completely lacks empathy. I am not for a minute suggesting they are a serial killer or any other kind of criminal. I am being descriptive not derogatory. I could simply call them non-empaths but since nobody knows what that means and 'psychopath' is pretty close to the mark, I'll go with that. Yes, there are negative connotations to the word 'psychopath' but I don't think it is a bad thing to use a word that suggests we should be careful around these types of people. This is one situation when it is definitely better to call a spade a bloody shovel.

Since I'm pretty certain empaths significantly outnumber psychopaths, I'll assume for the sake of discussion that you are an empath. If you're not, you've wasted your money. Psychopaths do not need strategies for coping with psychopaths. They are not confused by them at all. To them, every person is potentially either dangerous or lunch and how that person feels about their culinary status is irrelevant. No, this is a book for empaths. Empaths are the ones who need to know how to recognise, manage, work with and live with psychopaths. Empaths are the ones who need to learn how not to be lunch. And empaths are the ones who need to know how to use psychopaths to do good. A psychopath is like a piece of enriched uranium. Ignoring it or handling it badly can have horrific consequences. But if you are careful and design the system containing it well, it can produce enormous benefits.

Some very public examples

Below are some examples of behaviour from public figures to illustrate the kinds of activities I'm describing. I am not saying these people are psychopaths, but many other people have made claims about them in the public domain. These claims are not properly conducted professional diagnoses and I am certainly in no position to decide whether they are true or not. They simply help to illustrate the possible behaviour of psychopaths without me boring you to death with endless case studies about fictional characters called Nigel and Jane.

Saint Teresa of Calcutta (Mother Teresa)

Born Anjezë Gonxhe Bojaxhiu in Macedonia in 1910, Mother Teresa was an Albanian–Indian Roman Catholic nun. She moved to India as a missionary of the Sisters of Loreto when she was nineteen and taught in a school run by the order for two decades, eventually becoming the principal. In 1950 she founded the Order of the Missionaries of Charity, which managed homes for people dying of AIDS, leprosy and tuberculosis as well as running orphanages and schools. She won the 1979 Nobel Peace Prize. At the time of her death, in 1997, her order had opened 517 missions in more than 100 countries. She was posthumously made a saint by the church in September 2016.

According to reports, two-thirds of the people approaching Mother Teresa's missions were seeking medical treatment, but it was extremely limited; no painkillers were ever supplied, there was inadequate food and hygiene was appalling. Many people died from easily treated injuries or disease. The missions were described as 'human warehouses' where the seriously ill lay on mats, fifty to a room, and waited to die. There were few trained medical professionals on the premises, and most of the staff were unqualified nuns and brothers. This was in spite of the fact that Mother Teresa's order had raised hundreds of millions of dollars to provide palliative care. She explained why that care was not forthcoming by saying, 'There is something beautiful in seeing the poor accept their lot, to suffer it like Christ's Passion. The world gains much from their suffering'. She had no such concerns for herself, arranging the best possible medical care in California when she had a heart attack in Rome in 1987.

When asked how the poor could make the world a better place she replied that 'they should smile more'. However she lived a lavish lifestyle and spent most of her time travelling the world in luxury (usually in private jets) away from her home city of Calcutta.

Teresa frequently lied about her achievements in public statements. She claimed for example that her mission in Calcutta fed a thousand people a day. Sometimes she said this was 4000, 7000 and even 9000. The reality was very different. Her Calcutta soup kitchen actually fed a maximum of 150 people a day, including all the staff. She claimed to have 102 family assistance centres in Calcutta but when researchers went looking for them, they found none.

A 1995 documentary by Christopher Hitchens, *Hell's Angel*, all but called Mother Teresa a psychopath. Many writers since have been less reserved with the label.

Caligula

Gaius Julius Caesar Germanicus (nicknamed Caligula, or 'little soldier's boot') became the third emperor of the Roman Empire at the age of twenty-four. He was an extremely popular successor to his great-uncle and adoptive father, Tiberius. This was mostly because he was not Tiberius, but he quickly earned popularity in his own right. He immediately increased military spending by handing out bonuses to the army. He cancelled treason trials that had been scheduled by Tiberius (against anyone he perceived as a rival) and recalled people who had already been exiled. He cancelled tax debts and put on public gladiatorial games.

The charm offensive lasted for about six months and then things turned decidedly nasty. He raised taxes, reinstated the treason trials and had some senators executed and others tortured. He started to kill off anyone he perceived as a threat including his fourteen-year-old nephew, his grandmother, his father-in-law and his brother-in-law. He also famously introduced the idea of feeding human prisoners to the lions in the gladiatorial games.

In the third year of his reign, he began referring to himself as a god and would often appear in public costumed as one of the Roman gods. He had the heads of statues of gods in public places removed and replaced with his own head. It is unlikely that Caligula actually believed himself to be a god, rather this was part of a campaign to undermine the Roman Senate, by removing all checks on his power. Ancient historians describe Caligula as being an angry, callous, self-absorbed emperor who killed without compunction and enjoyed keeping his subordinates in abject fear. For example, during a banquet he would order the wife of a patrician to his room, where he would rape her. He would then return with her to the dinner and discuss her sexual performance with the guests.

It's hard to diagnose someone two millennia after they died but some historians are satisfied Caligula was a psychopath and not insane or psychotic.

Donald Trump

Donald Trump is an American real estate developer who became the President of the United States in January 2017. Before that he was best known for a reality TV show, *The Apprentice*, in which he would winnow down a pool of applicants for a job as his apprentice. During his career, he has built office towers, golf courses and casinos as well as lending his name to many other developments.

During the 2016 Presidential election campaign and since, many people have been prepared to suggest Trump is a psychopath. Former Obama aide David Plouffe told CNN, 'Basically, you have a psychopath running for president. I mean, he meets the clinical definition'. Tony Schwartz, the co-author of Trump's autobiography, told the *New Yorker* that if he were writing *The Art of the Deal* today, he'd call it 'The Sociopath'.

Lance Armstrong

Lance Armstrong was a professional cyclist who was at the start of a promising career when in 1996, at the age of twenty-five, he says he was diagnosed with a potentially fatal testicular cancer. After his recovery he formed the Lance Armstrong Foundation (now the Livestrong Foundation) to help other cancer survivors. He once again competed in professional cycling events from 1998 and won the Tour de France seven consecutive times from 1999 to 2005. He had been the subject of doping allegations since his first win in 1999 but had persistently denied doping. In 2012, a US Anti-Doping Agency investigation found that, over the course of his career, he had been the ringleader of 'the most sophisticated, professionalized and successful doping program that sport has ever seen'. At first Armstrong denied the claims but in August 2012 he chose not to contest the doping charges and was stripped of all race achievements since 1998. In 2013 he conducted an interview with Oprah Winfrey in which he confessed that some of the allegations were true, but he declined to provide evidence about the full extent of his drug use.

During the interview, Oprah put to Lance that he was a 'bully, sociopathic, only obsessed with yourself'. His only response was 'narcissistic'. Oprah confirmed that he felt he had behaved narcissistically, to which he responded 'Got it'.

Frank Andreu was a close friend of Lance's as he rose through the professional cycling ranks before his diagnosis. Betsy is Frank's wife. Betsy maintains that when Armstrong was recovering in hospital from his surgery, he admitted to her that he was doping. Betsy refused to keep his secret and spoke out against him at every opportunity for the next decade. For her trouble she faced constant vilification from Lance calling her 'crazy', 'jealous,' and 'psycho' while he tried to hide the doping he later publicly admitted to. In 2015 Betsy described Lance as 'a self-interested sociopath, a conman, and a manipulator'.

CASE STUDY: WAS GANDHI A PSYCHOPATH?

Psychologist and popular writer on psychopathy Kevin Dutton has been conducting an interesting study of the level of psychopathy for famous politicians. He has been asking biographers to fill out a psychological assessment on behalf of the people they have written about. Biographers have to get close to their subjects and know them in detail. Dutton used an abbreviated version of the PPI- R test, developed specifically for use in non-criminal populations and based on the answers to fifty-six standardised questions. The questions ask the person to say how they would behave, so having it completed by someone else is not a scientific test. Still, it came up with some interesting results. Here's how some leaders might have scored:

Score	Person	Score	Person
189	Saddam Hussein	155	Winston Churchill
178	Henry VIII	153	Napoleon Bonaparte
176	Idi Amin	152	Hillary Clinton
171	Donald Trump	136	Margaret Thatcher
169	Adolf Hitler	129	Bernie Sanders
165	William the Conqueror	123	Abraham Lincoln
157	St Paul	119	Mahatma Gandhi
157	Jesus		

Unlike many psychopathy tests, the PPI-R test has no distinct cut-off for psychopathy. However Dutton suggests that men scoring 155 or above have 'notably high scores' for characteristics associated with psychopaths. The same goes for women scoring higher than 139.

Allowing for gender differences, Hillary Clinton scored about the same as Donald Trump and they both scored higher than Adolf Hitler. Now that is a sobering thought.

I suspect Winston Churchill, Jesus and St Paul would not be on most people's lists of psychopaths, but it raises an interesting point. Psychopathy is not necessarily a bad thing for the group containing the psychopath. Having psychopathic characteristics does not necessarily mean you use them for evil against your own people. Sometimes the aims and needs of the group will align perfectly with the aims and needs of the psychopath. Context is important. Some researchers on the evolution of trust famously put it this way: 'Selfishness beats altruism within groups. Altruistic groups beat selfish groups. Everything else is commentary.' I suspect we could just as easily say psychopaths beat empaths within groups but groups who co-operate (as only empaths can) will always beat groups who don't.

PSYCHOPATHS ON SCREEN

The chap wielding the knife in Hitchcock's 1960 blockbuster, *Psycho*, was **Norman Bates**. But was Norman a psychopath? A recent study of film depictions of psychopaths concludes he wasn't.

According to the researchers, forensic psychiatrists Samuel Leistedt and Paul Linkowski, Bates was too delusional to qualify. They reckon he was more psychotic (being a 'socially functional misfit with a sexually motivated compulsion to kill') than psychopathic.

If you're after a realistic portrayal of psychopathy, the researchers say your best bets are:

Anton Chigurh, *No Country for Old Men*. The researchers describe the hitman as having an 'incapacity for love, absence of shame or remorse, lack of psychological insight, inability to learn from past experience, cold-blooded attitude, ruthlessness, total determination, and lack of empathy', which makes him a terrifyingly realistic portrayal of a classic criminal psychopath.

Gordon Gekko, *Wall Street*. A hitman is a bit of an obvious example of what most of us think when we hear the word psychopath. The less obvious, but significantly more dangerous, corporate psychopath is well portrayed by Gordon Gekko. Perhaps rather disturbingly, the director and writer of *Wall Street*, Oliver Stone, says that the character was based on several actual stockbrokers, including his father, Louis Stone.

Surprisingly **Hannibal Lecter**, *Silence of the Lambs*, didn't make the cut. The researchers found that he was too crazy. They thought the combination of exceptional intelligence, sophistication, charisma, erudition, civility, and wit disguising his cannibalistic nature was exceedingly unlikely to occur in real life (and I really hope they're right).

2

EMPATHY: THE MISSING ELEMENT

As I set out in the last chapter, my theory is that the psychopath's defining feature is a lack of empathy. So what is empathy? And why do most of us have it? The word empathy is quite a new word in the English language and is a translation (using ancient Greek roots) of the German word *Einfühlung* (feeling into). *Einfühlung* was first used by Robert Vischer in an 1873 doctoral thesis (*On the Optical Sense of Form: A Contribution to Aesthetics* – yep, it's about architecture not people). But Edward Titchener, a British psychologist, was the first English speaker to use the term to refer to people. In a lecture he gave in 1909, he used 'empathy' to describe what he called the 'full sympathy' of a psychology experimenter with his subject. And that's not a long way from how we use it today. The current dictionary definition is 'the ability to share someone else's feelings'.

Cognitive empathy and Theory of Mind

There is little doubt that most of us empathise with – share the feelings of – others. When we see a person in pain or afraid or happy, we feel it too. Perhaps we don't always feel it as intensely as they do, but we do feel it. But we are not born empaths. Or, put a more controversial way, all babies are psychopaths. It takes us a full two years to display the behaviours that indicate we are responding emotionally to those around us. A one year old can understand that other people have goals and can begin to simulate the other person's possible responses. And one year olds have a good enough understanding of what motivates others to attempt to predict their actions and even deceive them, but they don't appear to have true feelings about others yet. And while the signs are there by two, it isn't until the age of four that scientists agree a person's empathy is fully fledged. The average two or three year old can pass a Theory of Mind test (see over the page). Theory of Mind means they can understand another person's motivations, see things from their perspective and predict their behaviour accurately. By then the average empath child can run a simulation of the mind of another person and use it to automatically and accurately predict how they are likely to behave.

Non-human animals don't run Theory of Mind simulations. A human child knows that when you point at an object you are asking them to understand that you find it interesting and that they should look at it. Most people can't help but look. You can easily troll large groups of people by simply standing in the street and looking at the sky. You'll soon have a crowd looking up with you. Try it next time you're out.

Now try doing that with your favourite dog or cat. Point at a tree and see if your pet looks at it. They didn't, did they? Now try it with a human. Yep, they looked, didn't they? That, in its simplest form, is a direct test of Theory of Mind. Unfortunately, Rex (or Fluffy) failed.

Testing Theory of Mind

One of the most common Theory of Mind tests is called the Sally–Anne Test. In it the child being tested is shown two dolls (Sally and Anne). Sally has a basket and Anne has a box. Sally also has a marble, which is placed in the basket, and then Sally (with the assistance of her human controller) leaves the room.

While Sally is out of the room, Anne moves the marble from the basket into the box. When Sally returns to the room, the child is asked where Sally will look for the marble. If the child says she will look in the basket then they have 'passed' – that is, they have correctly predicted how Sally will react based on the information they know Sally has.

The child of course knows exactly where the marble is but to pass the test they must be able to simulate Sally's state of mind. Most four year olds pass this test. Down's syndrome children can too but Asperger's children usually fail it.

ASPERGER'S SYNDROME

Hans Asperger was an Austrian paediatrician who authored over 300 published papers on a condition that he called 'autistic psychopathy'. Asperger's description of the autistic psychopath was first published in 1944 and included five major features: a lack of empathy, social awkwardness, intense absorption in a special interest and a lack of humour, but otherwise having normal personality and intellect. The condition he identified received almost no attention in academic circles until after his death in 1980.

People with Asperger's syndrome have normal intellectual and language ability and development but have difficulty with cognitive empathy. This means they struggle to read the non-verbal cues in a social situation. For example, they can't tell that you don't want to hear their detailed explanation of the inner workings of the garbage disposal unit. And this makes them prone to banging on about their favourite subjects way past the point most people would have stopped.

Because they can't read emotions in others, they take what is said literally. They are tone-deaf to slight inflections in our voice and micro-expressions that tell others whether we are being literal or not.

Also, because they can't put themselves in the other person's shoes, people with Asperger's are often regarded as disrespectful and rude, but usually remarkably honest. Similarly, they have little ability to judge when something they say might be embarrassing to another person.

They are, however, well aware of other people's reactions to their behaviour. Because of this, many work out rules designed to ensure they react appropriately (such as forcing themselves to make eye contact when they speak to someone). In a social situation, they have to decide on an appropriate reaction rather than it coming automatically. This often results in them coming across as stiff and awkward. It also means socialising is exhausting work for the person with Asperger's.

If you're having trouble picturing how someone with Asperger's might behave think of Sheldon Cooper, a character in the popular US sitcom *The Big Bang Theory*. Even though the creators of the show deny the character was modelled explicitly on the condition, he has many of the same attributes.

Asperger's syndrome was included in the fourth edition of the DSM in 1994 and then deleted in the fifth edition (published in 2013). People with those symptoms are now diagnosed as having Autism Spectrum Disorder. There is still significant controversy about whether Asperger's and autism (a large array of conditions which usually involves significant delays in cognitive and language development) are related conditions, but for now, people with Asperger's syndrome are generally diagnosed as having autism.

People with Asperger's syndrome are often accused of being psychopathic in their lack of empathy. The reality is, however, that while both psychopaths and Asperger's lack empathy, they are polar opposites. People with Asperger's lack cognitive empathy but have plenty of emotional empathy. They can't read us or predict our behaviour but they can feel our emotions. They feel we are angry or hurt or happy but they have no idea why. They also feel these emotions intensely within themselves and have trouble controlling their expression. Psychopaths, on the other hand, do not feel these emotions at all but are very good at telling when we feel them.

Emotional empathy

Empathy is more than just Theory of Mind – understanding what another person thinks – it is *feeling* it. Every psychopath I have ever met was extraordinarily good at knowing what I was thinking and even what I was feeling. Psychopaths are not weak in this department at all. They are intuitive and almost psychic in their ability to predict our behaviour. People who like to study such things (and there are many) call that 'cognitive empathy'. What psychopaths lack is the ability to *feel* our emotions. That ability to experience an emotion being felt by someone else is called 'emotional empathy'.

Theory of Mind (or understanding what other people are thinking) is clearly part of empathy but doesn't tell us whether there is an automated response to the emotions the person detects in another. Recent advances in brain imaging technology (which I'll get to in a moment) tell us that two different parts of the brain are involved in cognitive empathy and emotional empathy. Emotional empathy involves 'mirroring' – sensing a state of mind and automatically mimicking that state of mind for yourself. It's like a kind of telepathy. For example, you see another human feel anger, fear or disgust and, even if they say nothing, that feeling is transmitted to you and you feel it too. You subconsciously mirror the expressions they are displaying and, in turn, you transmit it to others. All of this happens without you giving it a moment's thought.

An empath responds to emotion in others on autopilot. Our reaction is instinctive and completely beyond our control. To do that, we must have fully functioning cognitive and emotional empathy. By the time the conscious part of our brain is engaged, our automatic response is driving our behaviour and our responses. You cannot control an empathetic response any more than you could control your heartbeat or your leg reflex in response to a tap on the knee with a doctor's hammer.

As highly social animals, we are constantly and automatically attuned to the emotions and desires of the humans around us. We are emotionally plugged into a shared consciousness which automatically responds to the ebb and flow of those emotions and needs. But a psychopath has no sense of this. While they can certainly tell what we feel, they lack the automatic response to it. They must engage manual thought, think about what an appropriate response might be and then pretend that is their response. That gap in timing is almost imperceptible but many empaths detect it automatically. They rarely know what it is, but it is an intuition that makes them uncomfortable around psychopaths.

A recent study scanned brain function while subjects were looking firstly at pictures of people suffering serious threat or harm and then at pictures of people in everyday situations. When others were in danger, parts of the brain associated with movement and increased awareness lit up. This gives us a clue to the likely reason for the development of empathy in humans. From an evolutionary perspective, relatively weak and defenceless humans found safety in numbers. But we don't just hang around together; it seems we have also evolved invisible emotional signalling systems to make us even safer. Groups of animals that respond to danger on auto-pilot probably survive longer than those that need to arrange a committee meeting to decide whether to run away.

One downside to living in large groups is managing the intra-group dynamics. Humans have needed to evolve an aversion to killing each other if they are to survive. It turns out that empathy is a critical part of what stops us treating each other as the enemy.

LACK OF CONTAGIOUS YAWNING
IS A SIGN OF PSYCHOPATHY

Yawning is contagious. We often yawn in response to seeing or just hearing another person yawn. Even reading about it can cause us to yawn. Go on, admit it, you just yawned, didn't you?

Scientists have known since the 1940s that yawning is contagious in humans and other social mammals (like apes and wolves). They have also known that the likelihood of us catching a yawn depends on the closeness of our relationship with the yawner. We are five times as likely to yawn if the yawner is a family member than if they are a stranger. Our yawn likelihood seems to be an excellent predictor of the depth of empathy we feel for a person. But even with complete strangers yawning is still contagious.

Research done in 2015 confirmed what many studies had previously hinted at. Contagious yawning is not just a sign of empathy. When it's missing, it's a sign of psychopathy. In the study, subjects were pre-tested for psychopathic traits and then exposed to pictures of people yawning. The researchers found that those who scored highest on psychopathic traits also scored lowest on the likelihood that they would 'catch' a yawn.

Remember though that psychopaths are excellent mimics, so don't go around giving them a free pass just because they yawned when you did.

How psychopaths react to emotional events

Most of us cannot perform multiple manual thinking tasks at once. If I ask you to tell me the product of 38 and 73 without using a pen and paper (or a calculator – put it away), I will have just about maxed out your manual thought systems. If something requiring an emotional response (say, for example, a news story about a terrorist attack) occurred while you were working the sum out, you would stop and respond to the news story. A psychopath wouldn't. If a psychopath is distracted by a task they can forget to engage their emotional simulator and their responses to emotional news can seem odd. This is because empaths have an autopilot response for emotions which is completely lacking in psychopaths. If you have ever seen a psychopath in action, you will probably have seen them make this mistake. You may be chatting to work colleagues in a group when one of them tells a story which is emotionally distressing, perhaps, say, about their child attempting suicide. If the psychopath is not paying close attention, they will blunder straight through that cue. While everyone else is visibly upset for the storyteller and their child, the psychopath might ask about an irrelevant detail (like how exactly did the child do it – did they slit their wrists across or up the vein?). Or they might just change the subject without skipping a beat. To the psychopath, information has no emotional weight. It is all just information. Telling them you like red cars has the same weight as telling them your daughter attempted suicide.

Interestingly studies of psychopaths have revealed that they focus better than the rest of us in general, not just when there might be emotional interference. Because part of them is not keeping watch for emotional cues, they can devote themselves entirely to the task at hand. They seem to be able to screen out input which is irrelevant to their immediate goal. In one study, when psychopaths were monitored playing a video game while an irritating beep was being played at random intervals in the room, it didn't bother them at all. But when empaths were put in the same situation, they struggled to focus on the game.

After a natural disaster, for example, empaths cannot help but respond to the TV coverage of human devastation and misery. We feel the suffering, we understand the loss almost as if it were happening to us and we want to help, even though we know none of the people involved. It is enough that they are people. In some cases we feel empathy for non-humans as well (usually as long as they are lovable and have a face like ours – no one really cares if a cockroach gets squashed in an earthquake). Psychopaths do not understand this at all. They feel nothing about the event other than that it is clearly affecting the empaths so they'd better look like it affects them too.

CASE STUDY: DONALD TRUMP AND 9/11

There would be very few of us who don't know where we were when the first plane struck the World Trade Centre on 11 September 2001. It is the kind of event that is burned in our memories by intense feelings of shock, grief and anger.

But it seems that none of these feelings affected Donald Trump at the time. Hours after the planes hit, Trump did a live phone interview with his former publicist Alan Marcus on TV. In the interview, Trump does not sound at all disturbed by what is unfolding on the screen in front of him in his home town. He doesn't sound upset or angry or suggest retaliation or speculate as to who was responsible. His responses are matter of fact. In answer to Marcus's concern

---

about 40 Wall Street, a 71-storey building owned by Trump near the twin towers, he says 'actually [that building] was the second-tallest building in downtown Manhattan, and it was actually, before the World Trade Centre, was the tallest – and then, when they built the World Trade Centre, it became known as the second-tallest. And now it's the tallest.' He went on to express disappointment that the stock exchange had been closed because of the attack.

We all respond to shocking events in our own way. And Trump's apparent lack of emotional response and his focus on irrelevant details does not necessarily make him a psychopath. However, this kind of response would be how a psychopath, who is missing emotional cues that so deeply affect the rest of us, might act.

What causes lack of empathy?

It's clear psychopaths don't feel our emotions (or largely, even their own), but once again the question is why? Why are there humans living among us who are completely divorced from the emotional world that consumes our every waking minute?

Until very recently the study of psychopaths has been firmly in the domain of behavioural psychology. Everything we know about them was obtained by speaking to them and watching how they behave in certain situations (and hoping like crazy they weren't just acting for our benefit). And, even then, most of the work was only really done in criminal populations. Unfortunately, none of that tells us what causes psychopathy. But that hasn't stopped people making some very big guesses. Everything from a violent childhood to exposure to pornography to genetic mutation have been put forward as explanations. Anyone claiming those were anything more than guesses is having you on. The result has been a consensus in the psychological and psychiatric communities that psychopathy is a description of a variety of personality disorders sharing the common theme of lack of empathy.

The majority view is there is no cure but that it is likely that a troubled upbringing is a big part of the reason the psychopath is the way they are. Unfortunately, evidence to back that up is non-existent. There is no doubt that many psychopaths would see the ability to blame a poor upbringing as a powerful weapon in their armoury of deception but that doesn't mean it's any more likely to be true than any other explanation. And, even where we know it to be true, the only closely studied group of psychopaths (people banged up for violent crimes) are unlikely to be terribly representative of the population as a whole. The reality is that most psychopaths have no idea why they are the way they are and they certainly don't think they are the ones with a problem.

All humans are born prematurely. Most other animals come out ready to function. A horse can walk immediately, a turtle can swim straight away and a baby dolphin can do calculus right off the bat (they are smarter than us, you know). Those animals are born fully formed. But newborn humans are what software engineers call 'minimum viable product'. We have to be because waiting any longer would mean we couldn't get that gigantic brain out through those narrow hips (a consequence of walking upright).

Human brains quadruple in size between birth and pre-school. And it isn't just their size that changes. Our brains are not getting fat; they are getting hundreds of times more complex. Pathways are constantly being built and rearranged right up until adulthood.

Our brain is our greatest and most flexible tool. Research has clearly shown that the pathways built in our brain are responsive to our environment. Our brain is a neural network which learns the best response based on what is happening in our environment. This gives us a significant and distinct advantage over creatures with fully formed brains and hardwired responses (what we call instincts). Increasingly, however, it is becoming clear that the developmental wiring has gone wrong with psychopaths.

CASE STUDY: TED BUNDY BLAMES PORN FOR PSYCHOPATHY

Theodore 'Ted' Bundy was perhaps America's most famous serial killer. Just before his execution on 24 January 1989 he confessed to killing thirty women between 1974 and 1978, after spending the previous decade denying he had killed any. Investigators believe the toll was much higher than the thirty he admitted to.

Bundy was intelligent, charismatic and good-looking. He used his attractiveness to approach victims in public and lure them to secluded locations where he raped and eventually killed them. He would often revisit crime scenes and perform sexual acts long after their death. He also hacked off (at least) twelve of his victims' heads and kept them as souvenirs. He later told investigators that he regarded his victims as his possessions.

Ted didn't have a white picket fence upbringing but it certainly wasn't terrible by any stretch of the imagination. He was born in a home for unwed mothers in November 1946, but lived with his mother and her parents until he was four. His mother then moved them to Washington state to live with cousins. Eventually she married

---

the man who became Ted's adoptive father. Even by his own account, Bundy had a happy childhood and adolescence.

He finished high school in 1965, enrolled in university studying Chinese in 1966, but dropped out a year later. After a few years drifting from job to job, he began studying psychology at the University of Washington, graduating with honours in 1972. He began studying law at the University of Puget Sound (now Seattle University) law school just a year later, but never finished the degree.

No one knows when he started killing women. He told one biographer he performed his first kidnapping in 1969 but didn't kill until 1971. He told a psychologist he killed two women in 1969, but told police his first killing was in 1972. Some investigators think he actually killed an eight-year-old girl in 1961 when he was just fourteen.

Bundy was arrested in 1975 but escaped several times before being arrested again in 1978 and sentenced to death in 1980. He was the subject of a large number of psychiatric examinations during his nine-year stint on death row. And it seemed as if the diagnoses were as varied as the people making them. **Bipolar Disorder** (manic depression that causes unusual shifts in mood, energy, activity levels, and the ability to carry out day-to-day tasks), **Dissociative Identity Disorder** (multiple personality disorder characterised by the appearance of at least two distinct and relatively enduring identities or dissociated personality states that alternately show in a person's behaviour) and **Narcissistic Personality Disorder** all registered as potential explanations but the consensus is that **Anti-social Personality Disorder** (ASPD, or what you and I would call a psychopath) is the best match. There was also a strong consensus that he was perfectly sane, not suffering any kind of psychosis and knew exactly what he was doing.

He frequently told FBI interviewers and doctors that he felt no guilt or remorse and accepted no responsibility. He was also universally acknowledged as being highly manipulative. One of his examining psychiatrists admitted 'sometimes he manipulates even me'.

To his very last hours on earth, Bundy tried to manipulate others. On the afternoon before he was executed Bundy granted his last interview to James Dobson, the founder of a Christian Evangelical organisation and a long-time high-profile campaigner against porno-graphy (he is also pro-censorship, anti-abortion, anti-divorce, anti-gay rights and anti-evolution). In the interview, Bundy blamed his crimes on an obsession with pornography and suggested that the FBI stake out adult cinemas and follow the customers as they left. The full inter-view was filmed and is available on Vimeo – do you believe him?

This was completely new. Just the night before, he had told the FBI investigating agent that porn had nothing to do with his crimes and that he had never had any real interest in it. Biographers now believe that the Dobson interview was one last roll of the dice; an attempt to gain an influential voice to campaign for his life by playing the victim to someone he knew wanted to hear that message. At the very least it was a way to blame something other than himself for his crimes.

The brain and emotions

In the early 1970s psychologists led by Paul Eckman decided to test out something Charles Darwin had noticed a century earlier. In his book *The Expression of Emotions in Man and Animals*, Darwin noted that all animals (including us humans) express fear in exactly the same way. We freeze in place and adopt a startled expression. Our heart and breathing rates suddenly accelerate. Stress hormones are released and we are significantly more likely to startle. Darwin went on to theorise that this remarkable consistency across individuals was likely to apply to all human emotions and likely to be the same across all human cultures. Eckman's studies set out to see if that was true.

The researchers showed photographs of various expressions to thousands of people from cultures all over the world. They found that almost everyone, regardless of location or cultural background, correctly recognised happiness, surprise, anger, disgust, sadness and fear in the photos they were shown. This was true even if they were told the expression was something else (for example, sadness or anger rather than fear) or the face was that of a person from a completely different culture.

Because of this remarkable consistency in our experience of emotions between species (as far as we can tell) and between cultures, it did not seem unreasonable to suggest that emotions were wired into our brain's structure and not just learned behaviours. Early experiments in animals (and eventually humans) have suggested that empathy, as well as emotions, live in distinct places in our brain. If those places are damaged, people start having an awful lot in common with psychopaths.

In 1939, Dr Heinrich Kluver, a German-born psychologist working at Stanford University in the US, was trying to find out which parts of the brain were affected by mescaline. Mescaline is an addictive hallucinatory compound extracted from cacti that are native to Central and South America. It induces a psychedelic state similar to LSD and 'magic' mushrooms. Native Americans have been 'tripping' with it for around 6000 years. Kluver had neuro-surgeon Paul Bucy remove the temporal lobes of macaque monkeys while they were alive to find out how mescaline did its work.

He didn't discover how mescaline worked but he did observe a series of changes in the animals once they recovered from the surgery. They all still had normal vision and motor skills (movement) but they all suffered from what Kluver called 'psychic blindness'. This he described as an inability to 'recognize the emotional importance of events'. They had profound amnesia (the inability to remember or to create new memories). They attempted to eat inappropriate objects (for example, rocks – so I guess that turned them into Labradors). They were not afraid of things that would frighten normal monkeys and they were hyper-sexual, seeking intercourse with just about anything that moved. They also became very placid when approached by humans; normal monkeys would make for the exits when humans came close.

Kluver–Bucy syndrome (as it was by then known) was first documented in humans in 1955. The affected people had temporal lobes removed or damaged because of accidents or disease (such as tumours or epilepsy). The primary symptoms in humans are the lack of an emotional response (often called the 'flatness of affect') and an inability to recognise faces or objects (for example, naming a pictured eagle as a 'robin'). By 1967 more monkey experiments had proved you could get the same effect just by removing the amygdalae (contained within the temporal lobes).

Where emotions live

The amygdalae (from the Greek word for almonds) are two almond-shaped (are you surprised?) bits of the brain located deep within the temporal lobes – the bits Kluver and Bucy were chopping out of monkeys.

Research in animals and humans has demonstrated that the amygdalae are bound up with emotions. In particular, this is where we process the fear we see in others' faces and where we learn to fear things that will hurt us. When Little Albert was learning to fear white rats, this was the bit of his brain doing the work. It is a powerful automatic learning process that is terribly useful in the real world. It is what teaches us very quickly not to touch hot stoves or walk barefoot through prickles.

A strong thread in psychology literature is that psychopaths are the way they are because of early physical or sexual abuse. But animal studies have shown that neglect and other stressful events *increase* the degree to which the amygdala responds to threats. And we know that in humans, early abuse is a significant risk factor for PTSD (post-traumatic stress disorder), a condition which is once again associated with increased amygdala responsiveness. Psychopaths have a decreased emotional response to threats and this is demonstrated by the decreased response of the amygdala. In this sense, PTSD is the opposite of psychopathy. PTSD sufferers are more emotional than normal. Psychopaths are less emotional than normal. This does not mean that psychopaths cannot have had distressing upbringings, just that this is unlikely to have made them a psychopath (and even less likely to cause them to suffer from PTSD).

The amygdalae are also involved in how we remember things. This part of the brain (the temporal lobe) is where we record things about our life. This is our automatic biographical memory, not the stuff we try to shove into our brain just before an exam. Psychologists now think that it is the amygdalae's role to charge our memories with emotions. This means that when we search our brain for memories, those that have the strongest emotions associated with them are the ones we find first. We will remember an event that was terrifying or otherwise emotionally charged much more easily than something which had no emotional connection because of the emotional hooks our amygdalae placed in our stream of memories.

Just like other parts of the human brain, there is rapid growth in the amygdalae after birth. The amygdala doubles in size by the age of two and then doubles again by the age of ten with most of that growth occurring between two and four. When Little Albert (aged nine months) was being taught to fear furry animals, the part of his brain that remembers such things was growing (laying down new connections) like the clappers. Little Albert was building connections in his danger-detection central processing unit.

The psychopathic brain

The psychology experiments on psychopaths described in Chapter 1 suggest that they don't experience fear like the rest of us. They seem to experience it but it does not motivate them the way it motivates us. If anything, it makes them more determined to battle on rather than run. Fear is an important emotion in normal human inter-actions. Real fear is hard to fake. Try it with a partner now. Tell them to look fearful. Whatever they do, I wager it'll look more like surprise or shock than fear. Real fear is the only way to produce an expression that would stop you in your tracks – and it would. A genuine display of fear by the victim in the face of an aggressive attack from a non-psychopath will generally reduce the likelihood of continued aggression. It signals to the aggressor that they have won and that it is appropriate to dial down the attack or call it off altogether. A psychopath's inability to recognise fear in others is very bad news for the person being attacked. The psychopath simply cannot detect that they have won until there is no doubt (because the victim is dead or otherwise incapacitated).

While the game-style psychology experiments described in Chapter 1 are suggestive, they are limited in their ability to tell us the true nature of the psychopath. The only definitive way to tell if psychopaths are truly different to the rest of us, or if they are just behaving badly because that's the way they roll, is to cut open their brains and have a look around. It would be even better if we could take a bit out and see what happened like Kluver and Bucy did with their monkeys.

Surprisingly potential psychopaths (and those medical ethics nit-pickers) aren't that keen on that form of diagnosis. But in 1978 a possible solution appeared on the horizon. Researchers working on defence engineering programs used strong magnetic fields to produce an image of a human brain – while the person wrapped around it was still alive. When neurons in our brain activate they consume oxygen, which is supplied by iron-rich red blood cells (haemoglobin). The researchers developed a machine with a magnet that aligned the iron in the blood cells while the imaging technology captured a series of rapid cross-sections of the brain. Those 'slices' show us which part of the brain is active, based on blood flow, at a given moment.

By 1986, the new technology (called Magnetic Resonance Imaging or MRI) had developed to the point that it could provide microscopic details about tissue architecture. By 1990, fMRI or functional magnetic imaging, the technology that allows us to look at a brain while it is performing a task, was invented. At the start of the twenty-first century it was possible (and increasingly affordable) to perform high-quality, detailed MRIs of brain structure and to do studies of brains reacting in real-time to stimuli (such as pictures).

The availability of MRI technology has revolutionised the study of all manner of diseases of the brain – everything from cancer to autism to schizophrenia. Critically, it has moved the study of psychopathy from the realm of informed guessing into hard science. For the first time, psychologists and psychiatrists can actually see the organ they are studying. It is having a similar impact to the invention of X-rays (the ability to actually see a broken bone without cutting someone open) had on the practice of orthopaedics (the study of our muscles and skeleton) a century earlier.

Functional MRI studies are now confirming that the inability to recognise fear in others is a genuine neurological deficiency and not just callousness. Psychopaths are no more able to feel fear in others than I am able to sing (believe me, I can't).

In a 2008 study Georgetown University professor Abigail Marsh decided to measure the degree to which psychopaths recognise fear in others. She put thirty-six kids aged between seven and ten into a functional MRI and showed them images of faces. The kids were chosen on the basis of their results on psychopath tests similar to the Hare PCL test discussed in Chapter 1. Twelve were at the psychopathic end of the spectrum, another twelve had ADHD (Attention Deficit Hyperactivity Disorder) and the remaining twelve served as normal (neurotypical) controls. Some of the people pictured had neutral expressions, some were angry and some were terrified. The researchers were monitoring something called the 'amygdala activation' in each child as they were shown the pictures. The kids who had previously been tested as having psychopathic tendencies had no real response in the amygdala when shown pictures of fearful expressions. But the amygdala activation of the ADHD kids and the neurotypical kids spiked when shown the same pictures. Psychopaths don't feel fear (as an emotion) or see it in others because the fear circuits in their brain just plain don't work.

Another MRI study on adults conducted in 2009 found that that difference in amygdala function could be detected as a physical difference in the amygdala itself. That study compared MRIs of twenty-seven diagnosed psychopaths with thirty-two non-psychopaths. The people were randomly selected from the database of a temp employment agency in Los Angeles and tested according to Hare's Psychopathy Checklist. (No, not everybody who temps is a psychopath, those are just the ones they found after they sampled lots of people.) Those that tested as psychopaths were matched (for age, gender, IQ, socioeconomic status, ethnicity, left-handedness, and history of alcohol and substance abuse) with controls who tested normal. The MRIs showed that, on average, the psychopaths' left amygdala was seventeen percent smaller than the non-psychopaths, and their right amygdala was nineteen percent smaller.

In 2012 a similar study performed structural brain scans on seventeen diagnosed male psychopaths who had been convicted of murder, rape and violent assaults, as well as twenty-seven violent offenders who were not psychopaths and twenty-two law-abiding non-psychopaths. In that study, the scans revealed that the structural differences weren't limited to the amygdala. The diagnosed psychopaths all had less structural grey matter than the other two groups in two front sections of the brain – the aPFC (anterior prefrontal cortex) and temporal poles.

The aPFC is the most recently evolved part of our brain and is roughly twice the size (relatively) of the same area in bonobo chimpanzees (the closest living relative of humans). We're still not entirely sure what it does (mostly because the technology doesn't yet have the resolution necessary to decode detailed information flows within the aPFC), but current research suggests it is involved in complex planning and reasoning. This is not a part of the brain that instinctively reacts like the amygdala; it is the bit that allows us to keep multiple goals in mind simultaneously and to run simulations of other possible scenarios. This is the impulse controller, the strategic planner and the considered decision-maker. And it was seriously underdeveloped in psychopaths. This might go a long way to explaining their lack of impulse control and how poorly they do when they sniff a reward. In the psychopath, the primitive reward-seeking amygdala overrides the more considered risk assessment of the aPFC.

The other underdeveloped bit was the temporal poles (this is just a fancy way of saying the tip of the temporal lobe). Like the aPFC, these are also relatively larger in humans and sit just below the aPFC. They connect the aPFC to the amygdala (contained within the temporal lobes). We know they are involved in social and emotional processing because a very common form of dementia results in the destruction of this part of the brain and the effects look similar to psychopathy.

FTD and the empathy neuron

Frontotemporal dementia (FTD) is second only to Alzheimer's in the number of people it affects. Around one-fifth of all early onset (younger than fifty) dementia is FTD. And while it is called dementia, it rarely results in loss of memory, language or perception. It is more a disorder of abnormal behaviour. It is caused by the progressive destruction of a special type of neuron (the spindle neuron) connecting the amygdala to the aPFC. Other neurons are not destroyed by the disease. The spindle neuron is only found in great apes (humans, gorillas, orangutans, chimpanzees and bonobos), some species of whale, dolphins and elephants. They are the same neurons in all these animals but there is a greater concentration of them in the human brain than in any of these other species. Recently, a more primitive form of the spindle neuron was also found in macaque monkeys. Macaques are the ones Kluver used in his experiments and are the most populous primate on earth, besides us. They also live in complex communities but with intense hierarchical organisation based on dominant matriarchal females.

The spindle neurons are relatively large cells which allow rapid communication across large distances in the brain. Scientists speculate that the spindle neuron is an evolutionary adaption to large brains and complex social groupings. They are tightly bound up with how we process social and emotional responses because they are the neurons responsible for transmitting signals from the amygdala (our central emotional processing unit) to the aPFC (our considered response unit). Recent work on the precise function of the neurons has described them as 'air-traffic controllers' for emotions. They transmit motivation to act and are particularly focused on adapting responses to errors to reduce the chances of committing the same error again. This capability is related to the development of self-control as a person matures and gains 'social insight'. MRI studies show us that these neurons are particularly active when intense emotions such as love, anger or lust are involved. But if you really want to see them light up, let a mother hear her child cry.

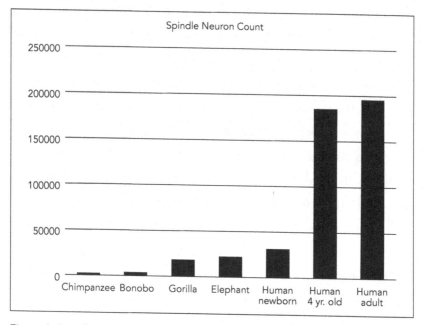

Figure 2: Spindle Neuron Count

The spindle neuron seems to be an important piece of hardware for big-brained animals that live in socially co-dependent groups. Some of the more advanced parts of these capabilities appear to have evolved in humans as recently as 100,000 years ago, more than 150,000 years after we became a separate species, and this either drove or caused our adaption to living in large communal groups.

Spindle neurons are developed relatively late as our brain grows. They first appear just before birth (at thirty-five weeks gestation), are very rare at birth, grow rapidly and seem to peak at eight months of age, before being trimmed back slightly to close to their adult level by four years of age.

In most animals precursors of these neurons are used to assist the animal's senses of sight, taste and smell, in part by helping it discriminate between edible and inedible. Human evolution seems to have co-opted the original function of these data transmission nerve cells. The human upgrade uses them to operate in a similar way but they also manage social interactions. Humans are still just as good as other mammals at smelling the difference between good and bad food, but most animals are much better than us at using smells to identify each other as well as predators and prey. It is likely that the reason our sense of smell is inferior to other mammals in this department is because we traded it in for the social upgrade.

The fact that spindle neurons also house our ability to discriminate visual and aural patterns provides an interesting biological explanation for some other psychopathic traits that have befuddled researchers for years. We have seen how psychopaths are terrible at recognising emotions in other people's faces and voices. This doesn't just apply to fear. A 2012 review of all the available studies concluded that they are uniformly bad at discriminating between emotions, positive or negative. Psychopaths are colour-blind when it comes to reading empaths' emotions as expressed in changes in facial expression and vocal tone. This makes sense once we know that psychopaths are light on in the neurons we use for pattern detection. It also means that their ability to 'read' us is based more on listening to what we say rather than how we say it. They pick up on our weaknesses and insecurities because we tell them about them, not because they have superhuman abilities to read our every thought.

In FTD, most of the spindle neurons are destroyed by the disease. This results in an almost complete loss of empathy, social awareness and social self-control. This is in stark contrast to Alzheimer's disease where the spindle neurons are not affected and none of those symptoms appear. FTD patients can no longer see things from another person's perspective. They also seem to lose any sense of morals. They no longer feel compassion, regret or shame although they still remain aware of their actions and are able to predict outcomes from their behaviour. In short, FTD patients behave like psychopaths. They retain the ability to tell right from wrong but have a slow and insidious loss of moral rationality. To re-use the term first coined in the nineteenth century, they become 'morally insane'. The progress of the loss of the neurons is directly proportional to the loss of all those capabilities.

Conversely, one recent study showed that having too *many* of these neurons results in increases in introversion, intense emotional awareness, negative self-analysis and suicidal behaviour. We are a finely balanced machine. Our ability to control our impulses, manage our emotions and empathise with others is controlled by these neurons. Too few and we become psychopathic; too many and we become depressed and suicidal. And these are capabilities we appear to develop or not develop in the first four years of life.

The moral insanity of FTD patients often leads them to behave callously and even in some cases criminally. Psychiatrists are quick to stress that FTD patients are not psychopaths but when pressed to say how they differ, the best they can come up with is that the crimes they commit aren't as bad as the crimes committed by criminal psychopaths. We do, however, know that more than half of FTD patients become involved in criminal behaviour. Those crimes include stealing, physical assaults, paedophilia and other sexual assaults. Sure, no one is aware of an FTD patient who became a murderer but that strikes me as the psychological equivalent of declaring that there is no such thing as a black swan after having examined 100 swans and discovering they were all white. Just because we haven't seen one yet doesn't mean they don't exist or haven't existed. It also doesn't mean that the psychopathic murderers we do know about weren't FTD sufferers either.

Criminal FTD patients are generally not suffering from any other form of psychiatric disorder. They are not mentally ill by any classic definition. They understand right from wrong, but they report that as they were committing the crime, they could not, or more accurately did not wish to, overcome the impulse to do the wrong thing. They knew what they were about to do to another person was morally repulsive. They felt the gut reaction we all would in that situation but it did not stop them doing it anyway. To me, that sounds exactly like a psychopath.

CASE STUDY: JOHN, THE FTD PATIENT

This is a description of a patient, let's call him John, whose FTD was confirmed by court-ordered testing.

John, sixty, was a former college professor with no previous criminal history. Since his mid-fifties, John's behaviour had changed significantly and had been getting progressively worse. He intruded into others' conversations and walked into offices that he had no business entering. He constantly stole things. In restaurants, he would fill his pockets with sugar packets and napkins, and at one point he had a collection of twenty-eight umbrellas that he had stolen. He ate indiscriminately, even going through waste containers and eating garbage. His increasing sexual demands of his wife, combined with these other changes, ultimately ended in their divorce. He then began stalking children.

He followed children home from school and tried to touch them. On one occasion, he put his arm around a young boy and then struck him when he tried to pull away. On another occasion, he stood at the foot of a pool and stared at the children for a prolonged time. When he exposed himself to his neighbours' children, he was arrested.

When interviewed, John denied having a sexual interest in children and there was certainly nothing in his past to suggest that this was not true. John did not deny his actions, could describe them in detail, and endorsed them as wrong and harmful. Despite this, he stated that he did not feel that he was causing harm at the time of his acts. He did not suffer from hallucinations, delusions or paranoia and his memory and ability to think in a linear fashion were normal, although he had a slightly less than normal ability to recall people's names.

According to the doctors assessing him, his lack of empathy and disinhibited compulsive tendencies driven by FTD explained his paedophilic behaviour. He was medicated but was not prosecuted.

IS THERE A SPECTRUM OF PSYCHOPATHY?

The short answer to this is: no one knows yet. MRI and autopsy studies on spindle neuron density are just beginning to appear but so far there is nowhere near enough data to tell us whether there is a sharp cut-off between normal and psychopathic or a spectrum of psychopathy. The best we can say is that studies so far reveal people diagnosed with FTD first start to show symptoms once they have lost about twenty percent of the spindle cells of normal controls.

In FTD patients we know that at some point they suddenly lack empathy, but who is to say that it wasn't just that that was when people noticed? A lack of empathy is a difficult thing to empirically measure.

We also know that psychopaths can be induced not to express their psychopathy (see page 164) and that could certainly make it look like one person is less psychopathic than another. But we have no idea whether that represents a real difference in the underlying brain structure or capacity for psychopathy.

I think the safest course is to simply assume a psychopath is a psychopath and any perceived difference is an accident of the circumstance in which you meet them. Being a little bit psychopathic is, I suspect, as likely as being a little bit pregnant. You either are or you aren't.

Psychopaths are Human 1.0

The existence of FTD leads us to a startling conclusion. It tells us that there is one biological structure which, when removed, takes away the empathy (and therefore morals) which lie at the core of what most of us believe makes us human. The base human condition may well be psychopathy. All of our species may have been psychopathic before we evolved those neurons a mere 100,000 years ago. Fortunately, as we began to enjoy the benefits of living in groups larger than a single family, our brain's circuitry evolved which enabled both empathy and impulse control. Human groups who mastered both were able to not just survive, but prosper and grow. The modern-day psychopath could simply be a glimpse into the past. It could be much the same as lactose intolerance – stick with me here, it's not as whack as it sounds. Societies exposed to milk as a source of adult food have evolved a tolerance for it over the last 10,000 or so years that span the history of cattle domestication. Societies that were not exposed (such as most of Asia) haven't and are largely lactose intolerant. The same thing has occurred with gluten, a protein found in the grains which have only formed a significant part of the human diet for the last 10,000 years. Could it be the same for emotional awareness? Societies that evolved the capability were able to dominate the planet. There may well have been societies where this did not happen but they have long ago succumbed to the forces of evolution.

Psychopaths are what we look like without empathy, morals and impulse control. We are self-aggrandising, narcissistic, selfish, unfeeling, amoral predators who care for naught but ourselves and how to advance ourselves at any cost. To an empath's moralistic eyes, psychopaths are the embodiment of evil, but to Mother Nature (and to other psychopaths), they are just another animal. We know that the required circuitry forms after birth and is complete by the age of four. If it fails to form there doesn't seem to be a way to force it to do so, at least after the age of four. For want of a better term, socialisation fails completely and those people without fully formed circuitry remain Human 1.0 – the version without the nifty social hardware upgrade. We don't know yet why it fails to form in some people.

THE RELATIONSHIP BETWEEN SPINDLE NEURONS AND SUICIDE

In 2011 researchers in Germany compared the density of spindle neurons in nine patients who died from suicide with thirty who died of natural causes. All of the subjects had been clinically diagnosed as either having schizophrenia or bipolar disorder. Within each group (suicide and natural causes) there was no real difference between the density of the neurons between schizophrenic and bipolar patients. But they found spindle neuron density was significantly greater (thirty-three percent) in the suicide victims than the others regardless of the underlying disorder. Higher spindle neuron density was strongly associated with suicide.

Perhaps it's a genetic propensity combined with a certain environment. Perhaps it's diet-related. Perhaps it's just the way some people parent or the degree to which children interact with others. We have no idea. And even if we did, what could we really do about it? I doubt there would be a lot of tolerance for early psychopath identification surveys of four year olds, let alone the (doubtless) pharmaceutical or (God forbid) surgical interventions that would be likely to follow.

DRUGS MAKE THINGS WORSE

Pharmaceutical companies know an opportunity when they see one. A drug that could cure criminal psychopathy would have an enormous market. They'd doubtless be able to charge an arm and a leg for one that worked. The direct cost of male criminal psychopathy alone was estimated in 2011 to be well over $460 billion a year in just the US. That was more than the estimated cost of treating obesity, smoking and schizophrenia combined.

Noting accumulating evidence that anti-depressant drugs can affect personality traits, researchers conducted a trial of this type of drug in ninety depressed patients between 1996 and 2003. The researchers assessed changes in the personality characteristics which are present (to a much greater degree) in psychopaths.

After eight weeks of drug administration they found that the patients' personality traits had significantly changed but not necessarily in a good way. The drugs increased social charm, fearlessness and social dominance. They also reduced impulsivity and the tendency to blame others for their problems. And while these were all good outcomes for the depressed patients in their studies, the researchers noted that a drug which could make a psychopath more fearless and more dominant was not likely to be a good result, even if it could make them less impulsive and less likely to shift blame.

The interesting aspect of this research is not so much its failure, but that it worked at all. In a roundabout way, it confirms the observation that depression and psychopathy are physiological opposites and that they are likely to be driven, at least in part, by the over- or undersupply of spindle neurons.

Unfortunately, the researchers also noticed that there was very little effect if the person tested higher for traits associated with psychopathy before the experiment started. So while these drugs might be able to suppress some of the emotional oversupply which characterises depression, it seems they can't repair the undersupply. Drugs can damp down emotional feedback but they can't create feelings or make a psychopath able to empathise.

PART 2

THE
EVERYDAY
PSYCHOPATH

3

RECOGNISING THE EVERYDAY PSYCHOPATH

Below is an excerpt from an interview with a successful corporate psychopath (Vaknin) about what a psychopath is:

Vaknin: *I like to present a facade of the self-effacing, modest person. It gives people the impression that, underneath it all, I'm human.*

Interviewer: *But you are human, aren't you?*

Vaknin: *I firmly believe that you want to believe that, yes . . .*
[The psychopath] regards people as instruments of gratification and as disposable things to be used . . . The vast majority of psychopaths, like an iceberg, are underwater, and like an iceberg, they are inert. They do nothing. They're just there. They torment their spouse by being unempathic, but they don't beat her or kill her. They bully co-workers, but they don't burn the office. They are not dramatic. They are pernicious. Most psychopaths are subtle. They are more like poison than a knife, and they are more like slow-working poison than cyanide.

Psychopaths are not all the same. Just like the rest of us, they vary in lots of important ways. Some are very intelligent and some are not. Some are good-looking and some are not. Some are men and some are women. Psychopaths are no more immune to cancer than we are and they are no better at football than I am. Well, all right, most of them probably are, but that's not because they are psychopaths, it's because I am uncoordinated. But one handy thing about psychopaths is that their behaviour is predictable. Anyone who has anything to do with one is probably staring in disbelief at the page right about now. Like me when I first encountered one, you probably believe that the last thing you could say about a psychopath is that they are predictable. That is true if you are trying to predict their behaviour based on what a normal person would do. Once you know that you are dealing with a psychopath, and adjust your frame of reference accordingly, their behaviour is significantly more predictable than yours. It just isn't what you would do.

Even though everything you are about to read would convince you that a person who behaved this way was the epitome of evil incarnate, psychopaths are not evil. Or, said more accurately, they are not *even* evil. They have no concept of right and wrong at all, but they understand that you do. They are not doing these things because they want to hurt you or cause harm. They just don't care if they do. Rather like a machine programmed to accomplish just one thing (see the Ava example in Chapter 8) they are pursuing their mission. To us, their callous disregard for others seems like the definition of evil but our judgement of evil is moral overlay manufactured entirely by our empathy (see much more on this below). Psychopaths have no way of experiencing what that is or why it is important. They see that it stops us making what they would regard as obvious decisions, but to them, that is just a weakness in our design, not theirs.

Key characteristics of psychopaths

In Part 1 I described all sorts of sophisticated definitions of, and tests for, psychopathy, but most of us can't get our boss to sit down and take a three-hour personality test. We'd also struggle to get them to shove their head in an MRI machine. We can, however, see and feel the impact of a psychopath.

To save you a lot of time on Google, the next section is a summary of all that I found online when I first began to suspect my boss. As I was reading article after article describing the same thing, I was ticking off all the behaviours occurring daily at work. It was extraordinary how closely my boss matched these profiles. It was almost as if they were written about him personally. I suspect that as you read this section you will come to the same conclusion about the psychopath in your life (yes, I am absolutely certain there is at least one in your life). Here's my list of key characteristics.

- Charming
- Self-obsessed
- Fluent liar
- Emotionally manipulative
- Completely lacking in remorse or guilt
- Emotional shallowness and callousness
- No responsibility for their actions
- Impulsive

- Parasitic
- Fearless
- Highly controlling
- Vindictive
- Aggressive and intimidating.

As well as that lovely shopping list of features, psychopaths are extraordinarily good mimics. They can read us like a book. They know our every desire and our every weakness within seconds of meeting us. They use that knowledge to reflect back to us exactly what we want to hear and see. It's why they are usually described as 'very charming'. That just means we like them because they look and behave exactly the way we like. It's probably not a surprise, given their ability to mimic us normal people (empaths), that we really have no idea how many psychopaths live among us. We have a pretty good handle on people whose psychopathic acts have landed them in prison (which is why they are there). Most researchers agree that between a sixth and a quarter of all prisoners are psychopaths and about a sixth of all substance abusers. But we really have no idea how many are in the wild. Recent estimates suggest it's around one in eighty in the general population and as many as one in five in senior executive ranks.

In the next section I describe the primary behaviours of psychopaths. I'll illustrate these behaviours with famous and garden-variety examples. This is not a checklist. It is possible to be an overbearing, bullying pig and not be a psychopath. But if a person exhibits all or most of the characteristics I outline below then there is a very good chance you are dealing with a psychopath and you should act accordingly (we'll get to what that means in practice).

Charming

'I sat down and took out my clipboard and the first thing this guy told me was what beautiful eyes I had. He managed to work quite a few compliments on my appearance into the interview, so by the time I wrapped things up, I was feeling unusually . . . well, pretty. I'm a wary person, especially on the job, and can usually spot a phony. When I got back outside, I couldn't believe I'd fallen for a line like that.'
– a story relayed to Dr Robert Hare by a woman
employed to interview psychopaths in prison

If you matter to them, psychopaths are charming, engaging and very interested in you. In fact they will usually be the most charming person you have ever met (or, at least, since the last psychopath). Because psychopaths are almost psychic in their ability to read your thoughts and emotions, they know what you want to hear. They will know instantly if you fancy them. They will know if you are worried about how you look in that outfit and they will know if you are nervous. They won't feel any of these emotions but they will know that you do (and they will see that as a weakness, but more on that shortly). They will seem charming because they will say exactly what you want to hear at that moment in time. Because they are untethered by moral boundaries they are frequently amusingly witty as well. They often push the conversation into slightly out of bounds and unexpected territory. They focus their whole attention on hearing what you say and responding the way you want them to respond. They will pump you for information and tell you almost nothing about themselves. Most of us are happiest when we are the topic, so we will think they are lovely company because of this. Most of us come away believing the psychopath to be one of the most charming and amenable people we have met in a long time.

All of this can come unstuck, however, when you meet the same psychopath in a group situation. Most psychopaths have no fear of public speaking. They will happily be the centre of attention for a large group of people. They don't, however, like engaging socially with a group of people who they don't know. Psychopaths tend to avoid loose social gatherings of strangers (or virtual strangers) so don't expect them to hang around at the work Christmas party for long.

Imagine you and four other people are standing in a group with a psychopath at a social function and the psychopath only knows you. The psychopath is presented with a feedback problem. If it were just you and she there, then she could reflect your wishes and desires back to you and you would get on like a house on fire, but in a group, she cannot possibly manage to reflect everything everybody wants to hear or see. Since her behaviour has to be manually controlled (see page 52), processing the correct feedback to multiple targets without putting any of them off requires herculean effort. To an empath this is just an easy, sociable way to pass the time. We react instinctively to the non-verbal cues – even from people we don't know – and we are not trying especially hard to reflect back what everybody wants to hear. But to a psychopath it's a dangerous marathon involving a lot of hard work. Dangerous because it involves a risk that they say something inconsistent with the image they have projected to you so far. And this might endanger the charm offensive that has worked so successfully to this point with you.

Psychopaths live in the moment. They will tell you what you need to hear now when they are charming you, and then whatever is most convenient to their plans when they are not. Because they have none of the machinery which supplies emotional hooks to our long-term memory, they struggle to remember details from the past. Their propensity to lie (see below) makes this even harder. We usually remember what we said because it was likely to be true and, if it wasn't, the trauma of lying probably stamped our timeline with an indelible mark. A psychopath, however, struggles to remember the lies they told because they have no emotional context for them.

CASE STUDY: STEVE, THE NEW CEO

Donna had just lost her husband of twelve years. He had suffered a heart attack while jogging. She was in a state of simultaneous grief, shock and panic. The panic was because Donna was now in charge of her husband's business. A business he had single-handedly turned into one of the most successful home-building companies in Brisbane. She needed help and she needed it fast. She was in no position to raise three young children and run the business, so she immediately advertised for a CEO. There were people within the company who could do the job but she wanted to see what else was out there.

There were thirty-two applicants but Steve stood out from the rest. He seemed perfectly qualified. He told her he'd run a similar-sized company in Perth but it had gone into liquidation when the owner was charged with fraud. Suddenly he was out of a job. His wife had left him when the company collapsed and so he decided to start afresh in Brisbane. He had an MBA from Sydney University and had worked for some of the biggest names in the building industry. Quite apart from all of that, he was charming and sociable. Donna felt special whenever she talked to him. Yes, he flattered her, and at times it was a little overdone. But she needed to feel good, and that helped. Donna trusted her judgement, so didn't check out any of his references or qualifications. She knew a good man when she saw one.

Four years later, Steve had forced her out of her company by turning the board against her. The move had taken her completely by surprise. Yes, many in the company had tried to warn her about Steve (usually just before they resigned) but he always had an explanation for any problem and she usually came around to the view that it was the person leaving who was the real problem.

She later discovered that Steve had never worked in Perth, had never worked for a building company, didn't have any degrees and had been fending off legal action from a previous employer in Melbourne when he took the job. But by the time she discovered all of this, it was too late. Donna had lost the business and was forced to support her children by herself. Becoming entangled with a psychopath often leaves a long trail of devastation for their victim.

Self-obsessed

'His campaign is all about him. How he treats other people is all about him – whether one is praised and patted on the head or cruelly mocked depends on what you have said about him.'

– Republican White House Aide Peter Wehner
referring to Donald Trump

Psychopaths need to be the centre of their environment and to utterly control it. If they have to choose between your adoration and your attention, they will go with attention every time. You don't have to like them but you do have to pay attention to them. This is a key difference between garden-variety narcissists and psychopaths. A narcissist (a person who can't get through a day without posting a selfie) wants you to love them. A narcissist will be devastated if you don't. Your adoration (or envy) is the motivation for their attention-seeking behaviour. To a narcissist, love and adoration *is* the end.

But, after a psychopath has charmed their way into your life, they don't much care if you hate them or love them. As long as you are focused on them that's all that matters. That focus gives them control over you. To a psychopath, narcissistic behaviour is a means to an end: obedience.

'Oderint dum metuant.'
Let them hate (me) as long as they fear (me).
– Caligula (Gaius Julius Caesar Augustus Germanicus)

In the psychopath's world, other people are one of three types: sheep to be fed and farmed until they are no longer useful; supporters who need to be flattered and cultivated until they provide something the psychopath needs; and enemies, people who must be destroyed if they get between the psychopath and their goal.

'NAS (a Caucasian, 85-year-old, twice divorced professional woman) was clearly aware of the ways in which other people tended to view her behaviour, but she was unaffected by their negative opinions.'

– findings of case study of 'NAS', a woman with Narcissistic Personality Disorder ('the NAS case study')

CASE STUDY: THE SECRET RUDD DIAGNOSIS

Two days after Labor lost the 2013 election, the *Australian Financial Review* reported on the existence of a secret psychological profile of Rudd which had been used tactically during the election campaign. Pamela Williams reported the Liberal Party had used the profile to predict Rudd's behaviour and design responses which would defeat him based on that behaviour.

When Rudd had been dispatched in 2010, members of his own party had been ruthless in their character assessment of his 'dysfunctional leadership' style and there was no shortage of people prepared to label him a psychopath. The Liberal Party had decided to seek professional help to arm them in a fight against such a personality. A psychiatrist friendly to the Liberal Party had diagnosed Rudd (from afar) as suffering from Grandiose Narcissism.

According to the latest version of the DSM, narcissists will have most or all of the following qualities:

- They are fixated on fantasies of power.
- They believe themselves to be unique and superior.

- They need constant admiration.
- They require obedience from others and special treatment.
- They will exploit others for personal gain.
- They lack empathy.
- They are envious of others and believe everyone else is envious of them.
- They are pompous and arrogant.

The document prepared for the Liberal Party reportedly zeroed in on Rudd's unshakeable belief that he is intellectually superior to everybody else 'on the planet'. 'Kick out that strut and he will collapse,' advised the report. The author said that the disorder would make Rudd obsessively paranoid and excessively vindictive. He would be extraordinarily sensitive to personal criticism. Any public challenge to his superiority could goad him into an uncontrollable tantrum. 'Later, in attempts to repair the damage, he will claim, in the calmest, coolest and most reasonable way, that his meltdown occurred because those around him are ganging up on him to prevent him from "saving Australia" or some other such grandiose concept. Kevin's explanation for the meltdown will run something like this: "Under the difficulties I face trying to save this country from the terrible threats facing it, any reasonable person would have naturally reacted the way I did." And then, blah blah, with grandiose ideas of being the country's saviour.'

The document suggested that Rudd's paranoia could be exploited. To that end, during the 2013 campaign the party stuck to a message that Rudd would be discarded by the Labor Party after the election. The diagnosis also drove the prominent assertion during the campaign that Rudd was full of 'flimflam'; suggesting he was all show and no go was aimed directly at feelings of superiority. The document also informed the Liberal line that Rudd's micro-management was generating chaos within the Labor campaign. The story ultimately proved to be true.

The Liberal Party machine, bolstered by the assessment, chose not to take Rudd on as he flitted from shopping mall to shopping mall to be mobbed by crowds of selfie-chasers. The assessment gave them the confidence to allow him to burn himself out. They knew that if the polls turned against him (as they expected they might after the honeymoon of his return as leader), his micromanagement and paranoia would accelerate and would ultimately destroy the structure and discipline needed for the campaign. The predictions were proved right as early as the second week, when reports emerged of unplanned announcements and unscheduled trips to destinations which no one in the team had prepared for. Rudd had taken control of the campaign. The massive Labor campaign HQ had been sidelined and decisions were being made on the run by Rudd, his family and a small team of trusted advisers.

The Liberal plan was simply to provide contrast. To be boring and predictable. Their candidate, Tony Abbott, was reduced to parroting slogans (such as 'We'll stop the boats' and 'We'll get rid of debt') rather than directly engaging with Rudd's antics. This was something the profile assured the Liberal Party would tempt Rudd into less than appealing behaviour. He might have a tantrum because he was not getting what he wanted when he wanted it. Or his confidence in his superiority would mean he might easily become a condescending know-all in the face of silence from the opposition. While Rudd dashed about from photo opportunity to thought-bubble announcement (for example, relocating the navy from Sydney to Brisbane), the Liberals were trying their best to look like the adults in charge and refusing to engage. It was an extraordinarily successful strategy. The Liberal–National Coalition won a landslide victory, benefiting from a seventeen-seat swing.

Fluent liar

'The very powerful and the very stupid have one thing in common: they don't alter their views to fit the facts; they alter the facts to fit their views.'
– Doctor Who

An inherent part of psychopathic charm is the ability to lie fluently. Psychopaths lie without any qualms. But they are still human and they still know that they are lying, so a lie-detecting machine is just as likely to pick up the physiological stress associated with a lie in a psychopath as it is in an empath. They are better liars simply because they get more practice. Empaths tend to start with the truth. We don't always end there but truth is where we begin. This is not how a psychopath thinks. To them, it is more important that you be told what they need you to hear than that it be true. A psychopath is completely detached from the need to remain truthful (or the consequences of being caught out in a lie – see 'Fearless' below). Their only limitation is that it is best to at least have a kernel of truth, because experience will have taught them that it is difficult to maintain consistency between lies and to remember what you said to whom, unless you have a thread of truth to hold it all together.

In my experience, when psychopaths are caught out in a lie, they rarely seem embarrassed. They just change their story or rework the facts (often with more lies) so they are consistent with the lie. You might think that would be complicated and it would just be easier to tell the truth but psychopaths have spent their whole lives lying convincingly. They are highly attuned to the concept of plausible deniability.

Plausible deniability is a concept used by intelligence agencies to disavow knowledge of operations which they expressly authorised. It is plausible because there is a lack of evidence linking the people making the direct decisions with those ultimately responsible. To a psychopath this means always having an alternative explanation at the ready: 'Oh you saw me out with that blonde last night? Yes, that's my sister from overseas.' Every time they lie, they are thinking in the background: if I am caught out in this lie, is there a plausible alternative explanation? This thought process ensures they build in just enough wiggle room to almost every lie they tell. Most psychopaths are proud of their ability to convincingly lie.

POLITICIANS' LIES

Two months out from the 2016 US presidential election, the *New York Times* decided it had had enough of being lied to by Donald Trump. The paper closely tracked Trump's public statements for the week beginning 15 September 2016. After culling statements that were false but could be jokes or rounding errors or just being said for effect, the paper had a list of thirty-one 'whoppers'.

The Pulitzer Prize winning political journalists at *Politico* took the analysis a step further, dissecting all statements made by both Trump and Clinton over five days starting on 15 September 2016. They found Trump had lied eighty-seven times. Unlike the *Times*, they didn't cut him any slack. They calculated this meant he lied every 3.25 minutes that he was talking. Talk to the man for an hour and you have been told over eighteen lies.

Clinton wasn't exactly a paragon of truth either, lying eight times over the same five-day period. Because she spoke less frequently that amounted to a lie every twelve minutes, or four times less frequently than Trump. Still, an hour with her would have netted you five lies.

Politicians wouldn't lie if it lost them more votes than they gained. The fact that they continue to do it confirms that we fundamentally accept many of their lies at face value. We want to believe they are telling us the truth, or at least, that the politician we like is telling us the truth. Sometimes, of course, we are just exhausted by all the lies and no longer care.

Dr Robert Hare once asked a criminal psychopath if she lied easily. She laughed and said, 'I'm the best. I think it's because I sometimes admit to something bad about myself. They think, well, if she's admitting to that she must be telling the truth about the rest.'

Sometimes the brazenness of the lie is what makes it plausible. An empath's reaction is 'he couldn't possibly be lying about something so obvious'.

As well as starting by telling the truth, we empaths also usually start from the position that we are being told the truth (because we assume everyone else thinks the way we do). We are, as a result, notoriously bad at detecting when we are being lied to. In experiments designed to test our abilities, most of us do no better than predicting a coin toss. Half the time we are right. Even the people who are paid to detect lies – like police, judges and customs agents – rarely do much better. So we are sitting ducks for a psychopath who has no problems manufacturing 'truth' to order.

Emotionally manipulative

A standard psychopathic tactic is the emotional outburst. This is one of the most disorienting aspects of working or living with a psychopath. One minute they appear happy with you and the next they seem upset by you, or worse (for some), they just ignore you. The empath expects that these emotions have something to do with what they have done and tries desperately to associate the psychopath's mood with their own behaviour. In fact, the display of emotion is entirely about what the psychopath is trying to achieve for themselves at that moment and has nothing to do with your behaviour or performance.

They will verbally, or sometimes even physically, attack you. If it is done in front of others, the purpose of the outburst is to isolate you and show others what happens to people who displease the psychopath. An empath would hesitate at doing this. A psychopath does not, however, fear any consequences and regards every person (besides themselves) as dispensable. As to explaining themselves, they will have a plausible reason ready to roll, should it ever come to that.

If the attack is done in private, its primary purpose is to remind you who is in control and to see how easily you can be manipulated by threats. Psychopaths are always looking for tools with which to manipulate you. Every insecurity you pass on to them will be used against you. If you are worried that a co-worker doesn't like you, that will be used as a lever against you. The psychopath might imply that the relationship could be repaired if you did A or B – both options that will benefit the psychopath.

Psychopaths like to test our ability to be manipulated very early in the relationship. They may feign an injury or illness to see how we react. If they think we are more easily manipulated by sympathy they will continue to use it as a tool.

CASE STUDY: PAUL – SYMPATHY AS A LEVER

Paul had had a glorious day-long first date with a woman. He could feel himself becoming attached to her, even though there was something slightly off-putting about her manner. Close to the end of the date, possibly sensing his hesitation, she explained that she was cautious about getting into relationships because of something

---

that had happened in her past. Worse than that, she said, when-ever she told a prospective partner about it, the new relationship quickly ended.

She told him that five years ago she had been engaged to a man who had committed suicide and she had been the one to find the body. It was extremely traumatic, she said, and broke down in tears, causing Paul to hug and comfort her. He went on to have a relation-ship with her, but ended it due to her continuous manipulations. He felt that her story (which he later discovered was a lie) had pushed him into a relationship that he probably wouldn't have pursued. And even had she not succeeded in gaining his sympathy, he felt like he couldn't have dumped her straight after she told him.

Psychopaths will also test our moral fibre. They will ask us to do something which we know is not right but for which there are limited chances of being caught or which won't result in any real damage. They might, for example, allow us to fudge a timesheet so we can go home earlier, or they might say something outrageous to see if we shut them down or laugh along. Every time we play along, they have added a bullet to their ammunition pile. Make no mistake, those bullets will be used against you.

Another favourite manipulative tool is secrecy. Psychopaths know that most of us are pretty good at keeping secrets, especially when we feel empowered by knowledge. Wanting to stay on the good side of our psychopathic boss, we often accept the secrets he passes on to us in confidence, especially if they are about someone we don't like much anyway. We love the implied intimacy, accep-tance and power. Psychopaths tell everybody different stories and swear them to secrecy. Each of these stories will be targeted to one of our insecurities. For example, if we are nervous about our place in the work hierarchy, they will tell us something that makes us feel secure while they secretly tell others we are on the way out.

Psychopaths know that if empaths are in emotional turmoil they will not be able to focus on the job. It provides a smokescreen for the psychopath to pursue their political or power-seeking aims without having to deal with the competition (who are by now all fighting each other or at least not on speaking terms). From above, the calm psychopath amid a sea of seething conflict looks like a person worth promoting.

Distraction tactics are not unique to individual psychopaths; they are increasingly becoming tools used by governments (who may or may not have psychopathic leaders). Chinese social media users have speculated for many years that comments supporting the government are posted by fake users. Users noticed that these posts and comments tended to appear in bursts around events that might cause public dissent, for example, the riots in Xinjiang province in 2013. The posts showered praise on the government and were generally highly nationalistic, exulting all things China. In 2017 a team of researchers, led by Gary King, a social scientist from Harvard, was able to analyse the phenomenon in detail. Their study found that the strategy was real and resulted in 448 million fake posts a year paid for by the Chinese government. After careful analysis of the content of the posts – cheerleading for China, the revolutionary history of the Communist Party, or other symbols of the regime – the authors concluded that the posts evidenced a highly organised strategy centred around avoiding arguing with sceptics of the governing party and the government, and to not discuss controversial issues. The researchers inferred that the goal of this massive secretive operation was instead to distract the public and change the subject.

Distraction is a favourite tactic of the psychopath. While we run around like headless chooks, they get on with furthering their own interests. Be wary when your workmates spend more time talking about why the new boss has changed the way expenses are claimed than they do about the fact she just got a pay rise for herself. Be wary when the media spend more time arguing about how many people were at Trump's inauguration than his conflicts of interest.

CASE STUDY: SAM, THE NEW BOSS ON THE JOB

A friend told me about the turmoil he experienced when a corporate change resulted in his team suddenly working for a psychopath (let's call her Sam).

'Sam gave a great first impression but things changed rapidly. Within days she was ripping up supplier agreements we'd had in place for decades, she was ignoring critically important customers to focus on other much less important (but more headline-worthy) deals. She also changed our expense-reporting systems and started challenging expense claims. They were all eventually paid but only after we fought tooth and nail for them. Then no sooner had last month's expenses been sorted then it started again. She was unrelenting in her apparent distrust of us.

'We all started spending a lot of time talking about what she was trying to achieve, rather than doing our jobs. We would talk for hours trying to come up with theories that made sense. But no sooner

---

did we think we had her figured out then she would do something else completely inexplicable. It was insanely confusing and distressing.'

My friend had almost forgotten about the fog of confusion and the distress it had caused him all those years ago, but it was all jerked back into sharp focus by the first few days of Trump's presidency. Like Sam, Trump tore up existing alliances, attacked allies and kept things unpredictable. And like my friend and his fellow employees, the rest of us have been running around like blue-arsed flies trying to figure out where we find this behaviour in the empathy rulebook.

Completely lacking in remorse or guilt

'Look, when you hurt somebody, you go to them and say, "I wanna show you how sorry I am. What do I have to do to make it right?" Instead, he doesn't do that. He doesn't do that with me . . . He doesn't do that with the millions of people out there who are disgusted and were swindled by him and gave money to his foundation. He doesn't do that. Instead, he does what he wants, for himself. How will this benefit him.'
– Betsy Andreu on Lance Armstrong

'She admitted to leading men on while using them for their money. NAS said that dating had been "a game" for her, but the men she dated did not see it that way. She claimed that several men left her house in tears after she rejected their marriage proposals; presumably, they viewed their relationship much differently than she did. Although she had clearly upset them, NAS said she felt no remorse for this, as it was "all part of the game".' – findings of the NAS case study

Psychopaths never feel real guilt or remorse for anything they have done. If harming you is something they need to do, then that is what they will do. They don't care about your feelings any more than you care about the feelings of your hair follicles after you've had a haircut. Do not expect remorse. If you think you see it, it is an act and the psychopath is attempting to manipulate you.

It is not unusual for a psychopath who has been found guilty of an offence or caught out in a lie to plead that 'shame is punishment enough'. It is not a punishment at all for a psychopath as they feel no remorse and could not care less what empaths think of them.

Unfortunately, since our entire legal system is based on the concept of punishment as a deterrent, it has no real power to change the behaviour of psychopaths. We know that criminal psychopaths are much more likely to manipulate their way into early release and, once released, are more likely to commit further crimes. The research tells us that the average criminal psychopath has been back and forth to prison three times before a non-psychopath with the same sentence makes it back once. Part of the way we learn is by fear of consequences (punishment). Part of this involves our internal experience of shame, humiliation and embarrassment. Psychopaths do not appear to learn from punishment and so shame has no power to shape their behaviour.

Emotional shallowness and callousness

'Peter is still around, but I know I couldn't get along with him. Ray said the other night that we should pack up his trailer

and head for South Carolina. I think I could get along
with him, but I really don't care for him. Jacob wants
me to make my mind up by Valentine's Day. With him
I would certainly have security, plus everything my little
heart desires. Jim said I could go to Oregon with him.
I told him I haven't tired of him yet. On the other hand,
I haven't seen as much of him as the others yet.'

– the NAS case study, extract from NAS's diary

Psychopaths do not experience feelings. If you see one looking like they are, they are lying. They know feelings exist because we all keep banging on about them. They know they can be used as levers to manipulate us. But they do not understand what an emotion feels like. To psychopaths feelings have the same status as colours do to a person who has never been able to see. They can describe them because they hear descriptions all the time. They understand they are important to others because they are constantly told about them or have things described using them. They have no direct experience of what it means to feel an emotion, but they know we empaths like to see feelings in others, so they get good at imitating them. If they ever forget to turn on the simulator, or just can't be bothered, we perceive it as emotional shallowness.

This emotional shallowness often comes across as an oddly jarring comment at an emotional time. Because psychopaths lack our automatic capacity to experience feelings in others, they make remarks which are perceived as callous and indifferent at times of emotional turmoil.

No responsibility for their actions

> 'The road to power is paved with hypocrisy,
> and casualties. Never regret.'
>
> – Frank Underwood, *House of Cards*

After the first Republican presidential debate in August 2015 Donald Trump implied he received hostile questioning and that the television moderator Megyn Kelly was menstruating. Trump said she 'had blood coming out of her eyes, blood coming out of her wherever'. He also called her a 'bimbo'. The closest he came to an apology was to say some nine months later, 'Did I say that? Excuse me. Over your life, Megyn, you've been called a lot worse, wouldn't you say?'.

Psychopaths believe they are perfect. They are incapable of believing they have done something wrong. Given this, they are completely unable to accept blame should their actions cause harm. They will admit blame if forced into a corner but as they are incapable of shame or remorse, these are just empty words.

Impulsive

> 'Boredom, and particularly the incredible circumstance of
> waking up bored, was the only vice Bond utterly condemned.'
>
> – Ian Fleming, *From Russia with Love*

Psychopaths are dopamine junkies, and this drives them to addiction and risk-taking behaviours. Dopamine is our get-ready-for-action hormone. When we anticipate food or sex (to name two of the more critical things we are supposed to stay interested in – from an evolutionary perspective), we give ourselves a squirt of dopamine. It sharpens us mentally, it improves our muscle performance and it speeds up our reactions. Similarly, when we are scared, dopamine is used to give us the best possible chance of escaping (or fighting, if we have no other choice). We can also make ourselves produce dopamine by consuming opioid drugs like amphetamines, caffeine and nicotine (and indirectly via sugar, but that's a story for a different book). And we can do it by purposefully placing ourselves in a stressful situation – otherwise known as extreme sports. Most humans like the way dopamine makes us feel so a lot of us go out of our way to get a hit. But that doesn't make us psychopaths.

We've known for a long time that psychopathic criminals are much more likely to abuse drugs and alcohol. And psychologists have long known that they tend to seek out risky activities for the buzz or to alleviate boredom. Psychopaths crave more edginess and risk than most of us could stand. A 2010 study from Vanderbilt University in Nashville, Tennessee, has gone a long way to explaining why. The MRI study monitored dopamine production in response to an amphetamine in known psychopaths and control patients. The result was stark. The psychopaths produced significantly more (four times as much) dopamine that normal people. They get a much bigger reward for their risky behaviour than we do. In a situation where an empath would feel a slight buzz, a psychopath is wired.

Psychopaths need constant mental stimulation. They hate the thought of a life where nothing is happening. But unlike easily bored empaths, they don't care if the buzz comes from positive or negative things. A psychopath will pick a fight to alleviate their boredom. But most empaths would avoid conflict. As long as something is happening, the psychopath doesn't much care about the consequences. And this makes sense when we understand that psychopaths don't fear or consider consequences the way the rest of us do. This often flows through into their sexuality. They are more likely to engage in sexually risky conduct, like engaging in multiple simultaneous sexual relationships without any of the partners being aware. They are also open to sexual practices which many people would find difficult to countenance, if not repugnant. They also frequently have quite fluid sexuality, simply following the most exciting option available at the time, be it male or female or both.

DO PSYCHOPATHS REALLY PREFER STRONG BLACK COFFEE AND G&Ts?

A recent study performed by researchers from the Innsbruck University in Austria found there was a strong correlation between people's preferences for bitter foods (like black coffee without sugar and tonic water) and their results on tests for psychopathic traits. Journalists everywhere pronounced that this meant anyone who liked strong black coffee or a gin and tonic was a psychopath and anyone who liked sweet milky coffee was a lovely sweet person. Millions of cafe patrons started looking suspiciously at anyone who ordered a long black, and denizens of licensed establishments began dodging the bloke ordering a G&T.

The researchers speculated that psychopaths preferred more extreme situations and picking the black coffee over the milky tea was the beverage equivalent of bungy jumping. I guess that's possible, but because this was a study by psychologists and not neurologists, I reckon they missed the more obvious explanation. Our evolved ability to discriminate between foods which provide energy (which are generally sweet) and those that might kill us (generally bitter) is driven by the exact same neurons as those scientists now think determine our levels of empathy. More empathy equals more ability to discriminate tastes (and smells and visual patterns).

A 2012 Australian study has tested how good psychopaths are at discriminating different smells. The answer is: terribly. They know they are smelling something, they just don't know what it is. The authors suggested that a psychopath's inability to discriminate between smells might (in conjunction with other tests) be a good spot check for psychopathy.

Given this, it's probably not so much that psychopaths prefer bitter tastes as that they are less discriminating. To a psychopath, black coffee and tonic water just aren't that bitter. Italians can breathe a sigh of relief. Your preference for a short black over a flat white doesn't (necessarily) make you a psychopath. It just means that you're Italian. Or from Melbourne.

The research also suggests that you are unlikely to find any psychopaths in professions that depend on a keen sense of smell or taste. So, if you want to avoid workplace psychopaths, wine-tasting is probably the job for you.

Parasitic

Psychopaths believe the world owes them a living and that the sole purpose of everybody in the world is to transfer rewards to the psychopath. It should, therefore, come as no surprise that they believe that a perfect human relationship is all take and no give.

In the workplace, the psychopath regards everyone who works for them as we might regard a herd of sheep, so it should come as no surprise that they see absolutely nothing wrong with taking the credit for anything the sheep produce. They see their job as controlling the sheep by using as little effort as possible. They do not see their role as improving the performance of the sheep nor as producing anything themselves. This of course makes them fundamentally lazy and parasitic.

CASE STUDY: JANE AND THE PETTY CON

Jane had spent most of her life exploiting her parents' sympathy for material gain. She was the youngest child of a family that included some very successful siblings. She had never tried to soar quite so high as them and instead liked to play the underdog card. So, when she decided she needed a car, there was only one thing to do. Her flatmate at the time relayed to me the extraordinary exchange that took place.

Jane rang her parents, who lived interstate and were quite wealthy but never extravagant. (Well, she rang and hung up after telling them to ring her back.) In the conversation that followed, she told a tale of woe about how one friend had been given a car by her parents, and how another had had a lotto win and bought a car,

---

while she was struggling to live in a suburban flat with only public transport to do the shopping. The guilt was ladled on with a spoon. After nearly an hour of this kind of moaning, which at times had Jane in tears, her mother said perhaps she could take her car, as she was thinking of upgrading. Jane would have to pay the registration and transfer fees though. The car was only worth the fees she had to pay. But when she hung up the phone, the tears instantly disappeared, a smile crept over her face and she said, 'Well, that's that taken care of', like she was ticking an item off a mental list.

Psychopaths enjoy the con, no matter how trivial. They love the feeling of putting something over someone for their personal gain. And this is true even if that gain is so pathetic that most of us just wouldn't be bothered.

Fearless

Psychopaths do not feel fear the way we do. They remain calm in the face of something that would cause us to run. This doesn't mean they can't have phobias (a type of anxiety disorder associated with avoidance of a situation or object). A psychopath is just as likely as an empath to have a phobia of spiders or heights. The difference is that they do not worry about it.

A psychopath cannot understand why we worry about things we cannot change or fear things that have not happened. And this goes a long way to explaining why the threat of future punishment does not stop them re-offending. They simply don't worry about the future, be it good or bad.

Psychopaths are the ultimate Zen human. They live in the moment. They have no anxiety about the future (despite what they might say) or any regrets about the past (despite what they might say). And they achieve this all the time, automatically.

The ability to remain calm when all around are losing their heads (with apologies to Rudyard Kipling) is a definite advantage in some situations. Some psychopaths have reported in blogs (which provide fascinating insights into their minds) that this calmness was often one of the first things that they noticed as being different about them as a child. In a dangerous situation, a psychopath does not back off out of fear.

Many people have suggested that this characteristic makes psychopaths the perfect soldiers. Perhaps that's why we still have psychopaths. Perhaps evolution has favoured groups who have psychopaths over groups who don't. Personally, I don't buy it. A psychopath may well be fearless but they will only look after themselves. Yes, they will face down a mugger but they will not protect you against that danger unless there is something in it for them. Yes, they will charge into battle but military units depend on every soldier being able to trust the man beside them. You cannot trust a psychopath to act in your best interests, only their own. They won't be taking a bullet for anyone, no matter how fearless they are.

DO PSYCHOPATHS KNOW THEY'RE PSYCHOPATHS?

Psychopaths know they are different. But they are no more likely to be able to label that difference than you are (until they read this book, of course). They know that they do not feel the emotions that many around them feel. They know that when most of us are horrified by a catastrophe on the news it doesn't affect them at all.

They know that they don't worry the way most people do and they have probably had occasions when they have not experienced fear when they should have.

For example, a person who was probably a psychopath told me that when bullies approached him at school, he knew he should have run away like his friends did. He had no particular fighting skills and would likely be severely injured by the bullies. But when fear should have made him run, he just stood his ground and bluffed. The more threatened he was, the more determined to stand and fight he became. He never had to fight. The bullies were put off. He also told me that if offered the choice between protecting himself or protecting himself and a friend, he would happily sacrifice the friend.

Psychopaths know this makes them different. They probably know this means they can exploit others' fears and emotions. But they probably don't have a name for it. And they definitely don't think there is anything wrong with them. Quite the contrary.

Highly controlling

'The controlling is very much an everyday occurrence. Complete interference with the minutiae of detail . . . [with what's] happening here and now, not involved in the vision, the five-, the ten-year strategic plan at all.' – from an interview as part of a case study of a psychopathic CEO in charge of a real UK charity ('the psychopathic CEO study')

Psychopaths believe they are the smartest person in the room. Always. To them, the occupants of any room they enter are, at best, barnyard animals. Obviously this means that no other person can be trusted to complete any tasks at all. They do, however, believe that if they provide detailed procedures and monitoring that most sheeple (that would be us) can be herded in the correct direction (being the direction which best suits the psychopath).

Obsessive micromanagement is a clear calling card of the psychopath. They will dedicate much more time to irrelevant procedures and processes than to substance. They will constantly add approval and supervision steps to all procedures. They will centralise all decision-making to themselves. And they will require constant reporting from all underlings. The massive centralisation and micromanagement serves two purposes for the psychopath. It allows him to control his possessions (once again, that would be us) and it provides a constant flow of information about his possessions, which he may be able to use to better control them.

We interpret micromanagement as a lack of trust in our abilities. Most people are insulted by, and react against, the type of micromanagement a psychopath implements. Psychopaths are not making any kind of judgement about your skills or capabilities. They assume you are a fool no matter what your experience or results, and no matter what they tell you. The psychopath will take credit for anything you do (you are, after all, his possession) and will ensure you are blamed for anything that goes wrong (rather like blaming the dog for that unfortunate odour in the car).

This does not mean that just because someone likes to dominate a conversation or a meeting that they are a psychopath. We are all capable of pushing our views forcefully.

The difference is that a psychopath will brook no discussion. They are not interested in your feedback and they assign no value to your opinions. If the feedback is negative then they will treat it as an attack and retaliate. Equally, a psychopath does not have to dominate a meeting. Frequently they are there simply because someone more powerful is in the room and they don't want any of their possessions talking out of turn. A friend told me her psychopathic boss would dominate staff meetings where everyone in the room was subordinate to her but would sit meekly at the back when her boss was in the room. But her presence, and the threat of retaliation (after the meeting) for talking out of turn, was keenly felt by all in the room (except the psychopath's boss).

Vindictive

'Some years ago, Mr Trump invited me to lunch for a one-to-one meeting at his apartment in Manhattan. We had not met before and I accepted. Even before the starters arrived he began telling me about how he had asked a number of people for help after his latest bankruptcy and how five of them were unwilling to help. He told me he was going to spend the rest of his life destroying these five people.' – Richard Branson

Psychopaths do not accept criticism. Remember, they consider themselves the smartest person in the room. If a psychopath appears to be accepting correction of any kind then the only thing that tells you is that the psychopath wants something from the person critiquing them.

If you were to complain to the psychopath about any of the characteristics I've listed in this chapter, they would treat your complaint as a direct attack upon them. They will retaliate against you. If you complain about micromanagement, you can expect to get more. If you complain about them yelling at you in public, you can expect it to happen more often. Complaining to the psychopath about their psychopathic behaviour is a sure-fire way to make sure you get even more of it.

'This particular issue came up and I said, "I disagree with you" to the (psychopathic) chief executive. He said, "Well I am making a decision on this." I said, "Well that's fine, I disagree with you." He said, "But you've got to agree with me because I am the boss." I said, "No I don't have to agree with you. I have to do what you say because you are the boss and you pay me but I don't necessarily have to agree with you and on this issue I don't." He slammed his hand on the table, raised his voice in the open office and said, "You have to agree with me" and then stormed off to his desk.'
– from the psychopathic CEO study

When dealing with psychopaths, you must be very alert to their ego. They see every action by every person as either an attack on their authority or obedience to their authority. You might think you are providing normal feedback, but a psychopath will treat any criticism (no matter how remote) as a direct attack requiring retaliation. Whether they retaliate will depend on your relative status, whether they think they can get away with it and whether they have time to retaliate. Of course, they may just do it to break the boredom.

Aggressive and intimidating

'When you're on the witness stand, we are going to fucking tear you apart. You are going to look like a fucking idiot . . .
I'm going to make your life a living . . . fucking . . . hell.'
Lance Armstrong to Tyler Hamilton at a Colorado restaurant, 11 June 2011. Hamilton was reportedly giving evidence against Armstrong to the doping investigation.

Everybody can react aggressively to provocation. We are all capable of impulsive aggression to some extent. But psychopaths are much more likely to plan and use aggression as a tool for furthering their interests. This type of ongoing aggressive response is a result of a failure to regulate their social behaviour and a disregard for the normal rules of interaction.

A psychopath will often use contrived aggression as a way of achieving extraordinarily petty outcomes. Say you are on the couch watching TV in a share house but the psychopath wants to spend time with her boyfriend in the lounge room. She will pick a fight with you about something she knows you are passionate about. It will quickly escalate into her screaming the house down, much to the embarrassment of all present (except the psychopath). Figuring nothing is worth the aggro, you leave in a huff. The psychopath then settles down (without any shame or regret) to enjoy a lovely time with her boyfriend. If the boyfriend is unsettled by the performance, she will give him some cock and bull story that paints you as a lunatic.

You will be mystified as to what just occurred, but to the psychopath, three important things have happened. They got what they wanted. You showed them a button to push. And you caved into aggression. They will not forget either the button or your weakness, so you can expect more of the same in the future.

Psychopaths' lack of impulse control and their highly manipulative natures make for a flammable mix when it comes to aggression. They will explode more easily than most and they will also use aggressive conduct to manipulate others. They know that most empaths will run from aggression if they can, and will be more easily manipulated if they can't run. They also know that most other people will turn away if they witness aggression towards someone else.

HOW PSYCHOPATHS CHOOSE THEIR VICTIMS

Criminal psychologists have long known that psychopaths have an extraordinary ability to select the most vulnerable people from a given group. In 2009 researchers from Brock University in Canada put this to the test. The trial involved forty-seven male students. The potential subjects were tested for psychopathic traits using a standardised test. Then they were asked to watch twelve videos of targets (eight women and four men) walking away from the camera. The videos had been taped without the knowledge of the targets. Half of the targets had a history of victimisation. The subjects were asked to identify which ones they were but weren't told how many there were. The subjects rated as psychopathic were incredibly accurate in their assessment. The non-psychopaths were far less accurate.

Later research by the team at Brock University found that the psychopaths were picking up on a raft of non-verbal cues. They noted the potential victims had several things in common:

- Victims had an exaggerated stride, either longer or shorter than usual.
- Victims walked slower or faster than usual.
- Victims' body movements were more backward and jerky. They lacked the fluid motions of the non-victims. In general, victims' body movements came across as disjointed and weak rather than confident and strong.
- Victims had a more slumped posture.
- Victims lifted their feet higher than non-victims.

How you'll feel when you encounter a psychopath

Victims of psychopaths universally describe the experience as being highly traumatic. Every person I interviewed while researching this book was keen to describe the psychopath's behaviour in minute detail as a warning to others. But none of them ever wanted to have any kind of contact with them again. They all asked that I never disclose their identity or the identity of the psychopath. They uniformly described a person who, on first meeting, was charming and personable. The psychopath came across as being someone with whom they were likely to have a good, even enjoyable, relationship. Within months, however, their personality seemed to change. The psychopath became cool, obtuse and at times unfriendly. Before long the relationship became dysfunctional. Many victims of psychopaths describe experiences similar to the following list:

- She became a **micromanager**. She started monitoring everything I did. I felt like I was being constantly watched.
- She became **incredibly critical** of me and did not allow me to make any decisions, no matter how small.
- There were many **'misunderstandings'**. I would believe that she had asked me to do something only to discover, after I had done it, that she wanted something else entirely. I was blamed for misinterpreting her wishes.
- Any **challenge to her authority** resulted in an immediate **backlash**.
- She had a **terrible temper** and would sometimes fly into a rage over the smallest thing. This would happen especially

if I questioned her about her reasons for doing something. The peculiar thing was that she could quickly turn the rage off and act as if it had never happened.

- She would also **occasionally praise and flatter** me. For those brief moments when I was on her good side I felt I must have been imagining my concerns about her.
- She would **frequently lie** about promises she had made to me. Or worse, deny that she had ever made the promise.
- I constantly **second-guessed my actions** and was unable to predict whether she would be pleased or upset with me. I felt like I was walking on eggshells around her all the time.
- She frequently made decisions which would affect me but **did not consult** me at all about them.
- Her behaviour dramatically **affected my confidence.** I felt worthless and like I was being crushed by enormous pressure.
- Having anything to do with her became a battle-zone where I needed to be **always on my guard.**
- There was **no one to talk to** about this as the longer I knew her, the less I had to do with others that had been part of my life before. **I felt alone.**
- No one else who knew her seemed concerned at all. Indeed, she **seemed very well liked.**
- I knew I wasn't **imagining all of this,** but at times it felt like I might be.

Yes, there are bad bosses, bad relatives, bad neighbours and bad partners (collectively, baddies) who aren't psychopaths, but psychopaths usually seem to follow a predictable path, very much like the one described above.

CAN WE SENSE THE PRESENCE OF PSYCHOPATHS?

Many women, my wife, Lizzie, included, say that certain people instantly give them the creeps. Often those people have subsequently behaved in ways which are suggestive of psychopathy. It has never happened for me but I have learned (the hard way) to trust Lizzie's radar. You don't have to read much about psychopaths before you come across stories about psychopaths making people's skin crawl. People say things like 'the hair stood up on my neck', 'he gave me the willies', and 'I got goose bumps'. But is it all just convenient anecdote? Maybe everyone gives Lizzie the creeps and she only tells me about the ones who turn out to be psychopaths, or maybe I only remember her mentioning it with those ones. Or maybe they were just creepy people in general and it has nothing to do with whether they were psychopaths or not.

In 2003 Reid Meloy from the University of California in San Diego decided to see if we really can detect psychopaths. In his study he asked 584 criminal justice and mental health workers whether they had ever experienced an involuntary physical reaction when interviewing known psychopaths. One hundred and twenty said they had never knowingly interviewed a psychopath. Over seventy-seven percent of the remaining 464 reported they had experienced an involuntary physical reaction in the presence of the psychopath. Females were significantly more likely to have experienced it than males. Eighty-four percent of females reported a reaction compared to seventy-one percent of males. Interestingly, police officers had the lowest percentage – just sixty-one percent reporting a reaction.

CAN PSYCHOPATHS DETECT PSYCHOPATHS?

Psychopaths are not superhuman. They have no greater ability to detect the presence of a psychopath than you do. The only difference is that they are usually actively looking for victims and you aren't (you aren't, are you?). The definition of a victim for a psychopath is someone whose emotions they can exploit. If the person the psychopath is evaluating gives no emotional response to the various hooks and baits they throw out, then they are not a potential victim. This probably means one of two things: either that person knows they are dealing with a psychopath and will not play along, or they are a psychopath themselves and can't be exploited. Either way, the psychopath will probably move on and (to use car theft as an analogy) find a car that isn't locked.

4

THE WORKPLACE
PSYCHOPATH

We all work with psychopaths. Sometimes they are our bosses. Sometimes they are our colleagues. Either way, it's a relationship that needs to be managed. In Part 3, I'll get into the nitty gritty of how to deal with them day to day, but first let's take a closer look at the types of jobs that attract them.

Do some jobs attract psychopaths?

'Psychopaths are social predators and like all predators they are looking for feeding grounds – wherever you get power, prestige and money you will find them.'
– Dr Robert Hare, Professor Emeritus of Psychology at the University of British Columbia, Canada and inventor of the PCL

As a general rule, a psychopath will be drawn to jobs which give them power over other people. Psychopaths believe they are superior to all other people and that the role of all other people is to deliver rewards to the psychopath. Add this to their prodigious ability to charm interviewers, and their complete freedom to make up whatever achievements they need to get the job, and it's easy to see how they may be fast-tracked. As a result, we can expect them to be towards the top of any corporate or political structure. The limited studies that have been done on the prevalence of corporate psychopathy bear out that assumption. The higher you go in any organisation, the more likely you are to encounter a psychopath.

Some jobs also give the psychopath power that extends beyond their organisation. No formal large-scale studies have been done which compare the occurrence of psychopaths by profession, but psychologist Kevin Dutton from Oxford University has been doing the next best thing. He has been steadily collecting data from an online survey called 'The Great British Psychopath Survey' hosted on his website. The survey offers to anonymously tell you if you are a psychopath. As part of the survey you must disclose your occupation. The results tell us that the professions most likely to attract psychopaths are (in descending order):

1. CEO
2. Lawyer
3. Media (TV/radio)
4. Salesperson
5. Surgeon
6. Journalist
7. Police officer

8. Clergyperson
9. Chef
10. Civil servant

Granted, it is a self-reported and self-selected survey, but it includes responses from over 3000 people and to me it looks about right. Every one of those professions rewards risk-takers, involves exercising power over others and, in many cases, requires subservience from others. They look like perfect career choices for psychopaths. The notable omissions to my mind are the two most likely to be at the top of the list: high-profile actors (and entertainers in general) and ugly actors (politicians). But given those two require almost perfect mimicry of empathy and feelings, perhaps they don't wish to be found out by filling in online surveys (no matter how anonymous they are meant to be). Or perhaps they have no need to fill in a survey to tell them what they already know.

Dutton's survey also reveals that the ten professions with the least numbers of psychopaths are:

1. Care aide
2. Nurse
3. Therapist
4. Craftsperson
5. Beautician/Stylist
6. Charity worker
7. Teacher
8. Creative artist
9. Doctor
10. Accountant

These professions are generally focused on catering to the needs of others. There's no luxury travel, mass adulation, excessive reward or power in being a nurse. That being said, these professions are clearly not immune from psychopaths. I have certainly come across a fair number of what I would regard as psychopathic teachers, doctors and accountants, so maybe, like actors and pollies, they are just more reluctant to fill in online polls. The survey tells us there are still psychopaths in these professions, it's just that there are generally less of them.

Psychopath or serial bully?

One of the most common euphemisms for psychopaths is 'bully'. But don't let the relative innocuous term lull you into a false sense of security. When the actions of bullies are broken down, the pattern of behaviour is what the literature describes for a psychopath.

The term 'serial bully' was first coined by Tim Field. Tim was a British computer programmer who became internationally renowned as an expert in delivering training to users with little or no knowledge of computers. Tim was bullied out of his job as a customer services manager in 1994 and experienced a stress-related breakdown as a direct consequence. This drove him to found a charity which ran the UK National Workplace Bullying Advice Line. The advice line gave counselling and advice to tens of thousands of victims of workplace bullying and, by the time of his untimely death from cancer in 2006, Tim had worked personally on more than 5000 bullying cases. His work inspired many similar anti-bullying organisations around the world.

Tim noticed that many bullying cases were caused by repeat offenders and that those people all shared a common set of character traits (see box) and patterns of behaviour. Tim described these people as 'serial bullies'.

TRAITS OF A SERIAL BULLY

- Jekyll and Hyde nature – Dr Jekyll is 'charming' and 'charismatic' while Hyde is 'evil';
- Convincing liar – makes up anything to fit his needs at that moment, and is believed;
- Treats some people in a way that causes them unprecedented levels of stress, frustration and fear;
- Damages the health and reputations of organisations and individuals;
- Reacts to criticism with denial, retaliation and by feigning victimhood and blaming victims;
- Apparently immune from disciplinary action;
- Moves to a new target when the present one burns out or leaves.

Yep, that's right. That's a pretty comprehensive list of the characteristics of the personality type that I describe as a psychopath. By 2001, Tim had formed the view that serial bullies were psychopaths. It was a view later endorsed by Dr Robert Hare, the inventor of the PCL.

In 2008, UK researcher Clive Boddy from Middlesex University set out to determine exactly how much workplace bullying was caused by psychopaths. He took a psychopathic checklist (similar to Hare's criminal version but without the questions about criminal history) and embedded it in a management survey of 346 middle and senior managers from multiple organisations in Perth, Australia. The checklist used a scoring system with a maximum score of sixteen (two points for each of the eight psychopathic criteria). Almost six percent of the respondents were working with a corporate psychopath (score between thirteen and sixteen) as their current manager and thirty-two percent had worked for a psychopath at some time. A further eleven percent of respondents were working with managers who showed psychopathic traits but were not rated at maximum in all categories (score between nine and twelve). Boddy called these people 'dysfunctional managers' but I prefer to use the term that most researchers do – moderate psychopaths. The remaining eighty-three percent were working for managers with a score less than nine and were therefore regarded as normal managers.

The respondents also revealed how many times they had experienced bullying (humiliation, sarcasm, rudeness, threats, violence or sexual harassment). Under normal managers, employees encountered bullying less than once a month (nine times a year), but the moderately psychopathic managers bullied employees more than twice a month (on average twenty-nine times a year), accounting for a twenty-one percent of all bullying. If that manager was a psychopath, the employee experienced bullying more than five times a month on average (64.4 times a year) and this accounted for twenty-six percent of all reported cases of bullying.

Combining these statistics, the study showed that almost half of all workplace bullying was done by the one in six managers with psychopathic traits and twenty-six percent of all workplace bullying was done by the one in twenty managers at the highly psychopathic end of the spectrum. When Boddy repeated the study in UK managers he found the rates were even higher. Thirty-six percent of all bullying was being done by the one in twenty managers who were clearly psychopaths.

This means that, as an employee, you can, and probably will, be bullied in the workplace. (If you aren't being bullied at all, why on earth did you buy this book?) If your boss is normal, bullying will happen once every six weeks or so. If you are working for a psychopath it will happen once or twice a week. For organisations, it means that just a few individuals are likely to be responsible for a large percentage of the bullying occurring in your workplace.

You might think I'm being a little heavy-handed describing workplace bullies as psychopaths. As far as you know, your boss has never committed one murder let alone a series of them. Surely, you may be thinking, bully, sociopath or narcissist are better words? I could call them that. I could pander to psychopaths by making them seem less dangerous if they have never been caught breaking the law. But this is not a book designed to help psychopaths wreck people's lives more efficiently. This is a book about knowing what you are dealing with right from the start. Forewarned is forearmed.

VOLUNTEER PSYCHOPATHS

Volunteer organisations are not immune to psychopaths. While they rarely have enormous amounts of money, they do provide a trusting environment that allows the psychopath to feed his ego and often put a little cash in his pocket at the same time.

Many volunteer organisations fundraise on a cash basis and rarely put financial controls in place. Who is to say the sausage sizzle made $1000 or $1200? Most empaths would be constrained by the moral repugnancy of stealing money from those they are trying to help, but a psychopath would feel no such qualms. Typically, they would recruit pawns to assist them in the deception. The psychopath may persuade the pawn that they are entitled to a free sausage or two for their efforts and over time this might grow to be a little 'reimbursement' from the till 'for their time and effort'.

As soon as a moral line is crossed, the psychopath knows a secret. Forever after, that secret protects the psychopath against being ratted out by the pawn if the psychopath is caught with the hand in the till. The pawn will fear disclosure of their secret but will probably justify their involvement in the deception as being compensation for all the work they put towards the cause. The psychopath will be telling them things like 'you work much harder and longer than all the others, it's only right that you take a little something for yourself'. All the while the psychopath will be taking much more for themselves.

5

THE PSYCHOPATH AT HOME

Sometimes the psychopath in your life is not at work. Sometimes they are your husband or your wife. Sometimes they are your brother or your sister or a parent. And sometimes they are your child.

Partners

I have never been in a romantic relationship with a psychopath. But many people close to me have. I am relying on my observations of their relationships in this section as well as one very precisely recorded account made after a relationship ended. The quotes in this chapter are from that account.

At the start of a new relationship be wary of the love-bombing. The psychopath will be the most engaging potential partner you have met in a long time. You will want to rush in. You will want to share intimate secrets. But you will find out almost nothing about them. Everything will move at high speed. Ask questions. Get background that you can check.

I don't mean be a sly stalker. I mean ask open, honest questions about their life and make a mental note for cross-checking later. We are all only separated from Kevin Bacon by six degrees of separation. You should be able to track down some common connection.

Your best defence against being charmed and rushed is to slow things down. I know that is easier said than done and we all get struck with 'fear of missing out' but if your connection is as real as you think it is, then an empath will stay the course. A psychopath may get bored and pursue an easier target. Don't be love-bombed into submission. The psychopath only wants you for what you can give them. And that is usually money and property.

If you decide to continue the relationship anyway, the psychopath will try to cut you off from any sort of support network. They will suggest outings that do not involve running into your friends or relatives. They will want you as their possession entirely under their control.

Over time you may start to notice some slips in the mask. This may unsettle you enough to make you leave, but if you decide to stay with the relationship, you must not tolerate lying. No, not even little ones. And you must not lie yourself. Do not be afraid of losing someone because you call them out on a lie. If that is the consequence, you have probably dodged a bullet.

You might, however, decide that there are enough positives about the person and the relationship, to justify you staying in it despite their obvious psychopathy. If you decide to stay, then you are deciding to suppress the harmful side of their psychopathy.

To do this effectively you will need to actively enforce honesty. And you will need to actively work on keeping lines of communication open outside the relationship. This means maintaining links with family and friends you had before the relationship and it means ensuring you and the psychopath socialise with those people together. It means ensuring you do the same with any people the psychopath associates with. You must also protect yourself financially. I'll go into more detail about all of this in Part 4.

If you start to think about leaving, the psychopath will sense you starting to disengage and they will love-bomb you again to keep you on the hook, or they may just bully you into staying – if you are still providing them with the lifestyle or attention they need.

Psychopaths are in a relationship with you because you can provide them with physical and, usually, financial security. They will be moving into your place. They will be using your car. They may even give up their job. You will be paying for outings and holidays. Their money will always be spent largely on themselves. You will be providing the joint experiences, money and property. In return you will get sex (but you probably won't be the only one) and love-bombing if you look like leaving.

CASE STUDY: PETER, PARTNER TO A PSYCHOPATH

I worked with Peter (not his real name) a while ago. We both eventually moved on to other jobs, but in a chance meeting, we got to discussing this book. He told me the story of the woman he had just been dating. He was absolutely convinced she was psychopathic. Here is his story:

'We would go out on dates and she would make comments like, "This is the best, I'm just putting it out there" or "This is the best Saturday night I have ever spent". It was very intoxicating.' Peter knew he was being charmed and that it was probably fake but it worked anyway.

'She asked me lots of questions about myself, but gave away very little about her past. For example, one thing she told me was that she had previously lived in Perth. I asked her when. She replied by asking when I had lived in Sydney. I said from 1996 to 1999. She said that was when she lived in Perth.' That was just one example of deflections that occurred constantly when Peter tried to dig into the detail of anything from her past.

'She was very, very complimentary about me and physically seductive, but I felt there was a complete absence of an emotional bond with her. It started to feel like a performance. I saw her lie in front of other people and put on a completely different face to what she told me her feelings towards the person were. Naturally, I wondered whether she was doing the same to me. She spent a lot of time sleeping because she said it was so exhausting putting on a performance for people.'

As I have discussed earlier, psychopaths wear a mask all the time, but it takes real effort to imitate our feelings. Peter felt he could tell when the mask slipped.

'I was ninety-five percent of the way towards leaving, and had in fact started to disengage. Then we were at lunch and out of nowhere she says, "Since the second date I thought I would marry you". Being someone who wants to get married, I thought maybe there was more to the relationship than I was seeing and that if she felt so strongly maybe I should give it more of a chance. Of course, in retrospect, she could see that she was losing me and needed another hook.

'More comments along those lines followed. My favourite was, "When we have children, I will have to have a clothing allowance". That turned out to mean that she had $50,000 in savings that she planned on using to fund extravagant clothing purchases and other financial self-love once she nabbed someone to take care of the mortgage. But she knew I also wanted to have children.' By now Peter was convinced she was a psychopath. But he still felt the tugs as she tried pushing emotional buttons she knew would work for him. Fortunately for him, he was prepared to walk away and that is exactly what he did. Although thinking back on the bullet he dodged still causes him to shudder.

Can psychopaths have long-term relationships?

Love is a feeling, so psychopaths don't experience it in themselves or understand it in others. But they are happy to exploit it for personal gain. If your love for a psychopath ensures you continue to provide whatever it is they need from you, then they will continue to pretend to love you and do whatever it takes to have you believe that is true. This may mean they have to suppress many of their psychopathic urges to keep you happy.

Psychopaths know what is right and wrong, they just usually don't care unless doing the right thing benefits them. They know they shouldn't sleep around, but if you don't find out or don't care when you do find out, they'll keep doing it. They know it's wrong to hit you or yell at you but if there is no consequence for doing it, they'll keep doing it.

And the only consequence that matters to a psychopath is deprivation of reward. If the psychopath is in the relationship because you provide, say, sex, money or power then those things must be removed if you want the psychopath to change their ways. Remember though that because a psychopath does not feel emotions they won't consider your love to be a reward. They are only satisfied by tangible, measurable rewards.

If a psychopath is in a long-term relationship it is probably because they have had to suppress their true nature (or most of it) in order to continue receiving the rewards that the relationship provides.

Are you in a relationship with a psychopath?

Relationships with psychopaths start out almost perfect, but quickly devolve into abusive exploitation that can ruin your life. Here are some signs you've partnered with a psychopath.

- **They were incredibly charming in precisely the way you liked to be charmed.** They mirrored your hopes and dreams. They loved everything you loved and were interested in all the same things you are. This also often translates into the bedroom. They know exactly what you want and are very focused on making sure you get it. Psychopaths are terrific lovers – at the start.
- **They identified and used your insecurities to make you like them more.** If you were shy, you suddenly felt like you became the most interesting person in the room. If you were overweight you were suddenly the most gorgeous person they had ever met. You felt special when you were with them.

- **They gained your trust early.** They shared detailed personal stories about their life early on. The purpose was to get you to share information about yourself.
- **They were impressive.** They told you stories of impressive performance in business and incredible success in general. Their air of confidence convinced you the stories must be true even though you didn't see anything to verify this. Sure, they drove a crappy car but that is because they really LOVED that particular model, not because they didn't have the money to buy a new one.
- **They manipulated your sympathy.** At the start, they had a story about a hard childhood, a bunny-boiling ex, a recovery from cancer, or something else designed to elicit sympathy in you. It was unlikely to be true and was probably short on verifiable detail. The purpose was to gain your pity and attachment. We are much less judgemental about people we feel sorry for and we are also much more likely to reveal our vulnerabilities to them.
- **They crave attention and surround themselves with fans.** Once you are hooked, they will start keeping company with other people – these are new potential partners. They do this to remind you that you are lucky to have them and that they have plenty of other options. As a result, you feel constant anxiety about your relationship.
- **They have no past.** You will rarely have been introduced to someone from their past or anyone who knows them from before you met. These people will not give good reviews so you are kept away from them.

- **They will sabotage and sever your relationships.** They will work hard to cut you off from your friends and family. They will purposefully work to make you feel uncomfortable around the people you used to feel most comfortable with. They want you to be dependent on them and loyal only to them. They do not want other people telling you your partner is a nutbag. They are jealous and they will actively exclude potential partners from your life.
- **They lie constantly.** Often when there is no reason to lie at all. But they always have a plausible explanation at the ready.
- **Nothing is ever their fault.** They are fantastic at rationalising their behaviour but never change it.
- **They straight out deny their own previous statements and behaviour.** They dismiss your attempts to present evidence of lies and, as a result, you often come out of a conversation with them doubting your own sanity. You will frequently be accused of being too sensitive.
- **They are parasitic.** You pay for almost everything. They will move into your home, not you into theirs. They will use your car. You will pay for outings. They will often need to borrow money from you.
- **You become yesterday's news.** Once they have hooked you, you seem to suddenly bore them. They give you the silent treatment and rebuff you for trying to rekindle the relationship you thought you had. They will sometimes disappear for days at a time with no contact and no explanation. They are usually working on the next conquest during this time or are simply two- (or three-)

timing you. If they sense this pushes you too far you will get a little more love-bombing to reel you back in.

- **You will be dropped like a hot potato.** When they have decided you are no longer of value to them, the relationship will be terminated like it never existed. You will feel isolated, insecure, insane, shocked and empty.

WHAT DOES AN EMOTIONAL HOOK LOOK LIKE?

When a psychopath first meets a new potential victim, they need to test them for exploitability. They will do this with an emotional hook aimed at gauging an emotional response.

They will tell us a tale of hardship that is in line with something they have discovered about us. For example, if they know we recently experienced a death in the family, then they might tell us that their beloved grandmother has just died and their grieving has been made worse by their crooked relatives convincing the grandmother to write them out of the will. If they know that we have an interest in improving the education system, then they may have a tale of how they suffered the most terrible abuse from teachers and parents as a child but managed to teach themselves.

The stories will be crafted to touch an emotional chord with you and to elicit your sympathy and compassion. It will not be overdone. If you respond sympathetically it will be a cue to the psychopath to push further and see how you respond. The stories will be convincing and heart-wrenching and any normal empath will find them compelling. If you respond with sympathy or compassion to the emotional hook, they have discovered a button they can press and they will have no hesitation using that to manipulate you in the future.

Psychopaths can be any gender

Most of the research I've mentioned so far has been concerned with male psychopaths. And almost all the research on psychopaths will tell you that they are much more likely to be men. But we probably need to take that with a shovel of salt. Most research on real-life psychopaths has been done on prisoners, almost all of whom were men. Which raises the question: are women less likely to be psychopaths or are they just less likely to be caught?

It reminds me a little of research I did for my book about education (*Free Schools*). Little boys are much more likely than little girls to be punished for bad behaviour at school. This is because when little boys misbehave, it is usually violent, disruptive and likely to present a physical risk to those around them. But when little girls misbehave, they are usually socially disruptive. A boy might hit another boy who has upset him and get detention for his trouble. A girl might exclude the offender from a social group instead – something Lizzie and I lovingly refer to as Grade 6 Girl Syndrome. Hitting another person is an immediate and obvious breach of the Golden Rule ('Do unto others as you would have them do to you'), our invisible moral code that stops most empaths from hurting others (much more on this in Chapter 8). Excluding someone from a social group probably doesn't qualify as a breach of the Golden Rule but it is no less damaging.

Researchers have found similar patterns in psychopaths. A male psychopath is likely to use overt physical violence whereas a female is more likely to use covert aggression aimed at damaging the victim's social status. This doesn't mean all Mean Girls are psychopaths, just that a female psychopath is likely to use the tools of her gender. So far there is no research that tells us there really are fewer female psychopaths, nor is there any known biological (or psychological) mechanism which would explain why there should be. The fact that most people think it's less likely just means women are probably better at hiding it. Women use manipulation because punching someone might get them seriously injured. Psychopaths use manipulation because it is easier to hide than physical violence. Psychopaths are never concerned about avoiding punishment but they are always concerned about avoiding detection.

CASE STUDY: THE BLACK WIDOW

In February 2009, Stacey Castor was found guilty of murdering her second husband, David, and attempting to murder her daughter Ashley. Ten years earlier Stacey's first husband, Michael Wallace, had suddenly started feeling ill. The couple had been married when she was just seventeen but they had grown apart after the birth of their two daughters. There were rumours they were both having affairs. Michael's illness grew progressively worse over a few months and, in early 2000, he died. Doctors diagnosed a heart attack and Stacey refused to consent to the autopsy demanded by his family.

In 2005, after just two years of marriage to David Castor, Stacey rang police saying her husband was locked in the bedroom and wouldn't come out. When police broke down the door they discovered him dead. Beside him was a glass of anti-freeze. The coroner found it was a suicide but a tip-off led police to search the house. They found David's DNA and anti-freeze on a turkey baster and Stacey's fingerprints were on the baster and the glass of anti-freeze.

The investigators then exhumed Michael Wallace, and found he had also died of anti-freeze poisoning. When Stacey discovered that Michael had been exhumed, she got her daughter Ashley drunk on vodka and prescription pain pills and typed out a suicide note which confessed to the murders of both Stacey's husbands. She left her daughter to die with the note but, fortunately, Ashley was discovered by her sister and resuscitated.

At Stacey's trial for the murder of David it also emerged that she had forged Michael Wallace's will to ensure she received his life insurance.

At her sentencing hearing, the district attorney sought maximum consecutive sentences noting she had 'partied in her backyard with friends like nothing was happening' as Ashley was comatose in her room. The judge said in his thirty-four years of professional experience he had 'never seen a parent willing to sacrifice their child to shift the blame away from themselves'.

Ashley told the judge she 'never knew what hate was until now. Even though I do hate her, I still love her at the same time. That bothers me, it is so confusing. How can you hate someone and love them at the same time? I just wish that she would say sorry for everything she did, including all the lies.'

A psychiatrist interviewed by ABC television in a documentary about the case said Stacey had 'psychopathic traits' because she killed for material gain and convenience rather than the sexual or sadistic motives which motivate serial killers.

Stacey was found dead in her cell in June 2016. The cause of death is unknown.

The screamer

One of the most tried and true manipulative tactics for psychopaths is the manipulative meltdown. Anyone can lose their temper when provoked, but what differentiates a psychopath is the tactical use of conflict to achieve an end. I have had close personal experience of this strategy being used in personal relationships. This kind of tantrum will come out of nowhere. One minute you'll be having a nice chat with your friends, when suddenly, for no apparent reason, the psychopath will fly into a rage. The purpose might be to divert the course of a conversation which was about to reveal something the psychopath didn't want told. Or it might be to get the psychopath's partner to decide it's time to go home. Or it might be to get empaths to back down on something they otherwise would have pursued (like who pays the phone bill in a share house for example). Once the aim is achieved, the psychopath will immediately revert to their charming mode – job done.

You might think this sounds like how a two year old gets their way. And that is exactly where the behaviour (and the expected outcome) is learned. Unlike the rest of us, however, the psychopath never grows out of it.

Depending on the circumstances, the micromanagement and bullying might take different forms (for partners, it might be reading your texts; for families, the fact the psychopath is always the last to decide on joint matters) but the intent is the same. The backlash might consist of screaming at you in public or excluding you but it will be real and the threat of it will always hang in the air.

Parents

CASE STUDY: NIGEL, THE PSYCHOPATHIC PARENT

Nigel was married to Sally for fifteen years. He contributed financially and was occasionally loving to Sally and their three children. Nigel also cheated on Sally regularly and was physically abusive to her and the children. Sally was an alcoholic and frequently absent in mind if not in body. Family life was chaotic. The family moved a lot and it was not unusual for the kids to discover there was no food in the house.

Nigel indulged the eldest child, Tom, but abused and rejected the younger siblings. Tom paid a price for the favouritism. He was expected to attend to Nigel's every need and desire without question. The whole family was also frequently verbally abused, even Tom. Nigel never did this in public though.

Nigel constantly lied. This usually involved him manipulating reality in such a way as to cause the family to doubt their own perceptions. He would often recall events in a way that portrayed him as a loving parent even though the children's recollection of the event was that they were abused or ignored. Even though Nigel was frequently abusive and often neglectful, he would constantly tell the children and Sally that he was devoted to the family and everything he did was for them.

Nigel would occasionally do things intentionally designed to cause fear in the children. Once he threw his thirteen-year-old daughter, Jane, overboard in a freezing lake on a fishing trip with the kids. Jane was forced to swim nearly a kilometre to shore. She was terrified but Nigel just laughed. All of the children were genuinely

---

afraid of Nigel and coped with it by developing a strong bond with Sally. But it didn't stop them blaming themselves for Nigel's abuse.

The children all needed and loved Nigel but were terrified by him. They were confused by his erratic ways. For most of their early lives they did not understand that his behaviour was not normal. As they got to know other families they slowly realised their father was brazenly antisocial. Even so, the children stayed in the family even as teenagers and young adults. They later described feeling like they were part of a cult, where the whole family conspired to keep its secret from the outside world.

Nigel's case study is an amalgam I created of the stories contained in seven published memoirs written by the children of convicted psychopaths. There is not a lot of research on how non-criminal psychopaths parent but we can imagine that the children will be love-bombed and manipulated when there is something in it for the psychopath. They will be used as tools of manipulation against the other parent. Or against each other if there are siblings. Or against the world at large if it is better for the psychopath's aspirations to look like they have happy children. The psychopath parent will probably not provide the children with expressions of love or any other emotion, except manufactured anger used to manipulate them. And the children's lives will swirl in turmoil and unpredictable switches between being ignored and being manipulated.

A psychopathic parent will most likely be neglectful, emotionally abusive and sometimes physically abusive, both to the other parent and to the children. This will be a stark contrast to the public face they present. To outsiders they will appear to be parent of the year, sacrificing their own wants and needs for their children, or at least sounding like they are.

To their psychopathic parent, children will be largely an annoyance that diverts resources away from the parent. They will have approximately the same status as the family dog. If they misbehave they will receive the same treatment as a badly behaved dog. They are both possessions that are malfunctioning. And the cure is punishment. Psychopaths abhor weakness in their possessions as they consider themselves perfect and weak possessions reflect badly on them.

Children

'[My] mother, the most beautiful person in the world. She was strong, she worked hard to take care of four kids. A beautiful person. I started stealing her jewellery when I was in the fifth grade. You know, I never really knew the bitch – we went our separate ways.' – Jack, a convicted criminal psychopath

A psychopathic child regards its parents and siblings as potential sources of financial reward. They will have learnt how to manipulate them very early in their life and will have constantly and relentlessly practised every day since. No one knows your weaknesses and hot-buttons more than your psychopathic child or sibling. They will expend much effort in schemes designed to manipulate family members against each other. Often this is so they gain some sort of privilege or even a financial reward. But sometimes it will just be practice.

They will use all of the manipulative techniques used by office psychopaths and a few more that will be specific to your family circumstances. If, for example, they know that it is important to you that you have time with your parents, they will ensure that last-minute emergencies or changes of plan constantly conspire to minimise that happening. They will partition family communication as much as possible so that suspicion is raised and trust is diminished.

CASE STUDY: MICHAEL, THE PSYCHOPATHIC CHILD

Michael started being difficult around the age of three, just after his brother Allan was born. He began throwing tantrums almost daily. They were much more extreme than the usual toddler blow-out. These five-star freak-outs went on for hours and would usually be a response to being asked to do something he didn't want to do.

By the time he was five, Michael was able to switch from tantrum to silky smooth charm at the drop of a hat. His mother found this deeply unsettling. This went on for years. At eight, Michael was punching the walls and kicking holes in the door or slamming the toilet seat down repeatedly until it broke. But he was also able to switch this behaviour off when it suited him. His parents tried every-thing – every expert and every recommended book – but they were unable to control him and unable to predict how Michael would behave. So, not wishing to take the chance of a public meltdown, they severely limited their social life.

Michael didn't care if his parents were mad at him. He would act out until he got whatever he wanted and was completely unrepentant. At the age of nine, Michael was diagnosed as being a psychopath by researchers at Florida International University.

Neighbours

CASE STUDY: JENNY, THE PSYCHOPATHIC NEIGHBOUR

Jenny dropped by to greet Anne and her husband, Mike, the day they moved in to their home. Jenny lived next door. She was friendly and charming and even helped unpack. She asked all sorts of questions. Some of them went a little further than the usual getting-to-know-you chat but Anne was keen not to start out on the wrong foot by taking a stand. And, anyway, she genuinely liked Jenny.

It wasn't long before things changed. At 3 am the following morning Anne was woken by loud music. It was coming from Jenny's place. Mike went over and asked her to turn it down. She did but only until Mike got back to bed, then up the volume went again. Mike called her this time but rather than apologise or turn it down, she turned it up. Mike called the police and eventually they sent a car. As soon as it arrived the music was turned down and as soon as it left it went back up again.

This was just the first in a constant stream of problems with Jenny. She would ring Mike at work (he wasn't sure how she got the number) to complain that Anne and Mike's dog was barking. She even called council inspectors around on three occasions. According to Mike, the dog is a house dog and never barks. Jenny set up cameras overlooking their house and told Anne she was recording because she knew they were stealing her pool chemicals. She would frequently toss rubbish and lawn clippings over the shared fence but deny it when confronted.

When Anne told other neighbours about this behaviour, they were perplexed. Most said Jenny was an ideal neighbour. Yes, a lot of different tenants had moved in and out of Anne's house, the only one which shared a boundary with Jenny, but the other neighbours had never noticed any problems. They had heard loud music every now and then but Jenny had told them it came from Anne's house. They struggled to believe that Jenny was anything other than a model neighbour. They had never had any problems with her and she was perfectly lovely whenever they saw her.

Like Nigel's case study, Jenny's is an amalgam I created from stories about psychopathic neighbours. In urban areas, we enter into an unwritten social contract with our neighbours. It is similar to the Golden Rule (see Chapter 8). We won't do anything to them or their property that we wouldn't want done to us or ours. Usually there are a loose collection of laws, regulations and body corporate rules that encode that rule to some degree, but most of us never need to have them enforced. Neighbourliness is an extension of our personal moral code. We stretch it to cover our homes and families too. Unfortunately, psychopaths have the same respect for the neighbourhood Golden Rule as they do for the broader Golden Rule.

Psychopaths behave exactly as they please and have no regard for your feelings about it. If they feel like having a heavy-metal party at 3 am then that's what they'll do. If their tree is dropping branches in your pool, then that's your problem not theirs. If their drains destroy your foundations, then once again, who cares?

Most empaths will attempt to take the high road in this situation. They will put up with the problem and hope it goes away. They may even politely ask the psychopath to stop. If they get desperate they may threaten to involve the body corporate, the council, the police or the courts. But to a psychopath, that is simply a demonstration of weakness. It tells them that you can be exploited. Worse, they will treat threats as an aggressive attack which will encourage them to counterattack. And when they counterattack it won't necessarily be through official routes. Psychopaths don't see the same boundaries we see. They don't see a bright line between right and wrong and they are not scared of getting caught. All they see is action and goal, moderated by plausible deniability. If you are someone they wish to attack, then yes, calling the police is an option, but a more direct option like disappearing your cat while you are at work is likely to be more effective.

PART 3

MANAGING
PSYCHOPATHS

6

HOW TO MANAGE
A WORKPLACE
PSYCHOPATH

Psychopaths are real people. They work with you, and for you, and could easily be your boss. In any given Anglo-Saxon dominated workplace there are probably more psychopaths than people with red hair (no, they are not the same people – well, not always). They exist. They are not a figment of a psychologist's imagination. They are not (usually) axe-murderers. They have not decided to be a psychopath. They just suffer from an irreversible failure of socialisation which impairs their ability to co-operate with other humans and which means they always act in a self-serving fashion without regard to the consequences. And while psychopaths certainly don't regard themselves as having a disability, that is no reason not to treat them as if they do. We wouldn't expect a diagnosed kleptomaniac (an obsessive compulsive disorder which involves impulsive theft) to perform work that involved unsupervised access to goods which could be stolen. We would ensure that their job matched their limitations and, where appropriate, we would modify their working environment to match those limitations.

A psychopath has a less obvious but no less real disorder. Once we understand that, we realise that if they are not effectively managed they will cause damage to the business, to us, and eventually to themselves. This does not mean they should be punished just for a lack of empathy (and all that entails). They are no more responsible for that than you are for being an empath. There is no cure for psychopathy and psychopaths neither want nor need our sympathy or assistance. In fact, it is dangerous for you to give it. But, for our protection and the good of society as a whole, they do need to be constrained.

Our challenge is to build those constraints for the workplace psychopath. I have three important tips on how to achieve that.

CONSTRAINING THE WORKPLACE PSYCHOPATH

1. Don't hire them.
2. Be alert to their presence.
3. Psychopath-proof your organisation.

Don't hire them

'It's better to have a hole in your team than an asshole in your team!' – Dan Jacobs, Apple Inc.

The best way to manage psychopaths is not to hire them in the first place. This is unfortunately a lot easier said than done.

A psychopath will typically look terrific on paper, largely because they have no qualms in embellishing their resume, leaving out negative experiences or just making positive stuff up. Due to their charm and ability to understand what you want, they will also interview very well. Even if they occasionally let the mask slip and expose a narcissistic trait, in today's individualistic society (see Part 4) that won't mark them out as being particularly unusual. Fortunately, there are some red flags to alert you.

THE VOIGHT-KAMPFF MACHINE

The 1982 science-fiction film *Blade Runner* depicts Los Angeles in the year 2019. In the film, humanoid beings called 'replicants' are genetically manufactured to do dangerous work in Earth's off-world colonies. The current version, the Nexus-6 (yes, that is where Google got the name of their Android phones), are identical to humans except that they lack empathy. Replicants are illegal on earth, so specialist police units, Blade Runners, are tasked with detecting and killing escaped replicants. The Blade Runners use Voight-Kampff machines to test subjects. The machine measures respiration, heart rate, blushing and eye movement as well as the emission of invisible particles in response to emotionally provocative questions. It usually takes twenty to thirty questions to determine whether the person is a replicant.

Since the defining feature of psychopathy is a total lack of empathy, the machine would also declare a psychopath to be a replicant (a plot hole not explored in the film). This, of course, would make the VK machine a handy little addition to the HR office. Unfortunately, they aren't real. But the test questions are and you can take the test yourself online at http://www.bfi.org.uk/are-you-a-replicant/. How did you go? Are you a replicant?

In 2003, a newspaper gave the VK machine test to all of the San Francisco mayoral candidates (without telling them why they were asking such odd questions) and found more than half of them – including the bloke who won – were replicants.

Look for frequent job changes

Tigers don't chase the herd all day long because once they are detected they have very little chance of catching anything. Similarly, psychopaths don't hang around once they are found out. This is partly because they lose the support of those above them, who up until then had been protecting them against the complaints of the people they exploited and manipulated, or they have destroyed the business entirely. Once a psychopath's patron forms the view that they have been duped by the psychopath, and that the psychopath is in fact the source of the workplace problems, the psychopath quickly moves on. So, be very cautious of a resume that has frequent job changes (one every two years or less).

Watch for unexplained gaps in their resume

Most people only leave a job once they have another job to go to (unless they were fired). A psychopath struggles to take responsibility for anything bad that happens, so if questioned about any unexplained gaps in their resume they are likely to tell a story about mass redundancies or the business going under. It will never be that they were fired for anything they did. Carefully check out (as best you can) any story you are told like this and make sure you have a reference from that employer.

Talk to referees

If the person you are interviewing is a psychopath, you will most likely be given reasonably good written references. If the psychopath left their last job before they were discovered (usually because the new job is a step-up) the reference will be from a patron. It will speak in magnificently glowing terms. It will speak of a person who is just this side of sainthood. A psychopath will have spent considerable time convincing the patron that they are the best thing since sliced bread and that will be reflected in the reference. If the psychopath left because they were discovered, the reference will be much more subdued, but it may still be positive. Often the organisation just wants them gone, and if a vaguely positive reference will help with that process then so be it. There may also be missing references. These are likely to be from organisations who abhor the psychopath and couldn't bring themselves to provide any support at all.

Obviously you want to speak to any organisation that doesn't provide a written reference but it's a good idea to speak to the others too. People are much more relaxed on the phone than they are in writing, especially if there is something negative to say. Real references about non-psychopaths usually contain some positives and some negatives but you come away feeling good about the candidate.

Thoroughly check qualifications and misconduct

Psychopaths have no problems inserting false qualifications often from hard-to-check sources. Do not assume any of the qualifications that influence your decision are real until you have verified that they are. Also check searchable databases which are related to misconduct warnings (for example, medical or legal professional databases).

The psychopath will leave those out of the resume. It is also a good idea to do a criminal records check. It is not at all unusual for psychopaths to have had brushes with the law. Lastly, run their name through Google. You might be surprised what comes up.

CASE STUDY: DR JAYANT PATEL – A LESSON IN RESUME CHECKING

Patel is an Indian-born, US-trained surgeon. In 2003, he was employed by Queensland Health as the Director of Surgery at Bundaberg Hospital on the basis of glowing references. He also signed a statutory declaration stating his license to practice had never been suspended or subject to restriction. But this was an outright lie.

In 1984, he had been fined by New York health officials for 'negligence, incompetence, and unprofessional conduct' and placed on three years' probation. Three years later, he moved to Oregon and, despite his record, obtained a job at the Kaiser Permanente Hospital in Portland. The interviewers were impressed by a glowing reference from a prominent New York surgeon which described Patel as possessing 'technical and professional brilliance' and being a man he would recommend 'without reservation'. He also claimed the New York proceedings against Patel were 'harassment of a brilliant young surgeon'.

In 1998, a US hospital restricted his license to practise due to persistent claims of malpractice. In 2000, the Oregon Board of Medical Examiners made a finding of gross negligence and made the restrictions statewide. A year later Patel was forced to surrender his New York State physician's license. A former US patient, John Dulley, who successfully sued Patel over his colon surgery, labelled him a psychopath.

During the two years he worked at Bundaberg hospital, Patel was linked to the death of eighty-seven patients. He was charged and found guilty of the manslaughter of four patients and served two and a half years in jail before the convictions were quashed by the High Court, which ordered re-trials. After the first re-trial failed to secure a conviction, the prosecutor dropped the remaining cases in exchange for Dr Patel pleading guilty to four counts of fraud relating to his registration as a doctor in Queensland. He escaped further jail time, receiving a two-year suspended sentence and cancellation of his registration as a doctor in Australia. The sentencing judge noted: 'I see no indication of, and I hear no expression of, genuine remorse for your offending.'

Be alert to their presence

Even with the best systems in the world, you or your organisation will inevitably hire psychopaths. Everyone needs to work, even psychopaths. So how can you uncover them in your organisation? The trendy term for the style of manager you are on the lookout for is a 'Kiss Up, Kick Down' (KUKD) manager. Psychopaths flatter and charm those that can hurt them and bully those that can't. If you don't ask the right people, you'll never detect them. Given that reality, here are some strategies you can use to uncover their presence.

Ask the right people

In 2006, psychologists Dr Robert Hare and Paul Babiak described the strategies used by psychopaths once they enter an organisation. They suggest that psychopaths divide the workplace into four groups:

- **Patrons** – people who have real power and influence and the ability to protect the psychopath from police and patsies.
- **Pawns** – people without any power or influence but who can be manipulated by the psychopath to support their aims.
- **Police** – staff in control functions like HR, audit, compliance and security who might get in the way.
- **Patsies** – once a patron or pawn is no longer any use to the psychopath, they turn off the charm and these people become discarded patsies. This usually only happens to a patron when the psychopath takes their job or to pawns when someone is needed to take the blame for something the psychopath has done.

After a short period of exposure to psychopathic tactics, the average workplace divides into two camps: patrons and pawns who support the psychopath; and police and patsies who detest them but are powerless to do anything about it because of the protection provided to the psychopath by the patrons. Every workplace psychopath I have ever encountered did exactly this. And to me, at least, the coalescing of these groupings within the organisation is a clear sign of their presence.

If I asked you your opinion of another empath you would probably highlight some positive things and some negative things and give an overall assessment that was neither particularly negative nor particularly positive. You might say – 'Lisa is a hard worker but often slow, so you've got to watch her on stuff with deadlines. But she's a great team player and really helps with the morale of the place.'

You won't hear assessments like that about psychopaths. People will either think they are the greatest employee since sliced onions or they are the devil incarnate. No one who knows them will have a wishy-washy opinion. The people below the psychopath in the corporate tree are the ones most likely to provide an accurate assessment. These are the people most likely to have seen the mask slip. Some of them will be pawns but some will also be patsies. If you get radically divergent opinions from people below the psychopath, then you probably have a problem.

Pay attention to sick leave

There are very real costs to employing psychopaths. Bear in mind though that the statistics reported in this section are likely to be significant underestimates. Banks rarely report the true level of credit card fraud because it makes us jittery about trusting them with our money. Similarly, most commercial enterprises don't like reporting on the existence or impact of psychopathy or 'bullying' for the same reason. They don't feel the need to air their dirty laundry in public.

Recent studies have concluded that people working for a psychopathic manager will be approximately twice as likely to take sick leave as those working for a normal manager. They are also twice as likely to take long-term sick leave. Estimates of the direct cost of this vary enormously because countries and companies differ a lot when it comes to who pays for sick leave. Many US companies, for example, don't pay employees when they are sick. But at the very least sick leave represents a significant drag on the productivity of a business. If sick leave rates are higher, and absences longer, than they should be, it means the enterprise is employing more people than it really needs. Productivity is also affected. One recent study calculated that this productivity drag amounted to 17.4 percent in Italian companies or, put another way, US$5236 per annum per employee.

In Australia, a study commissioned by a major health fund in 2007 revealed that the total cost to the economy of work-induced stress was $14.8 billion while the direct cost of stress-related absenteeism and presenteeism – being at work but not working – was $10.11 billion a year.

If your organisation's sick leave is blowing out and your productivity is dropping, then have a close look at the person who all the suddenly sick people work for.

It is not always the pawns who are sick though. If a patron who has been protecting the psychopath starts to have doubts, the psychopath may feign illness in an attempt to use feelings of sympathy (yours, not theirs) to protect themselves.

From the psychopath's perspective, pretending to be sick is an excellent way to avoid being fired – they can continue to draw down a wage, do no work and get everybody's sympathy. It is also a terrific delaying tactic. You never know what might change – the new boss might go under a truck, they might get a promotion . . . you just never know.

Psychopaths play empathy and sympathy against us. No matter how much we may doubt the veracity of their illness, we (and the boss) are unlikely to call it out or to move against the psychopath.

CASE STUDY: THE SICK PSYCHOPATH

A friend of mine tells the tale of when her psychopathic supervisor (let's call her Kathy) suddenly lost a patron. Kathy's boss retired and was replaced by a young go-getter. The old boss had been kindly disposed to Kathy and if not overtly protective then at least tolerant of her as long as the section kept producing the work. The new boss rode Kathy mercilessly and would not tolerate her usual blame-shifting tactics. Kathy's response was to immediately become ill with a non-specific ailment that prevented her putting in a full day's work and often necessitated work from home. Her desk was littered with medication and she would often be gone for days at a time. The sickness lasted for more than a year and no one was ever quite sure what it was.

Just like a cornered tiger might feign illness while waiting for a better chance to attack, a cornered psychopath will do the same.

Staff turnover

The most common response to a psychopathic supervisor is to leave. Unusual turnover rates are also one of the easiest data points for an organisation to measure.

The higher the psychopath is in the organisation, the more damaging staff attrition will be. If they are the CEO, they will eventually cause more competent managers to leave or they will target them for dismissal if they perceive them as competition. This inevitably results in whole tiers of experienced managers being obliterated. With no competent leadership from above, each successive tier below becomes less productive, less focused on the aims of the organisation and more focused on just keeping their job.

So if your organisation starts experiencing a high staff turnover, check your managers and supervisors carefully.

Lawsuits

Obviously if you suddenly find your organisation embroiled in an unusual number of lawsuits, particularly from staff who worked for a particular individual, or customers and partners who interacted with that individual, then it is time to take a closer look at that person.

Psychopath-proof your organisation

Whether you have a current psychopath problem or not, there are things you can do to ensure that when you employ a psychopath – and inevitably you will – your organisation represses and controls psychopathy, rather than encouraging it. If you achieve that you will simultaneously become less attractive to other psychopaths and better able to manage the ones you have.

Culture of honesty

> 'The standard you walk past is the standard you set.'
> – Chief of Australian Army, Lieutenant General David Morrison, in relation to the Australian Army's culture, attributed to David Hurley

> 'Ten years ago, people would have said that there were no ethical issues in business. Today employees think their number-one objective is to be thought of as decent people doing quality work.' – Norman Augustine, CEO of Martin Marietta (later Lockheed Martin), after the successful implementation of their corporate honesty program

The best place to hide a body is in a massacre and the best place to hide a lie is in a place full of liars. It is much harder for psychopaths to use lies to their advantage if everybody else is honest. Cheating is also harder to get away with if you're the only one cheating.

Dishonesty in the workplace costs the average business five percent of its turnover. Cutting back on dishonesty obviously helps claw back some or all of that money, but more importantly, it helps discourage psychopaths. For example, it is very hard for a psychopath to get dirt on someone by looking the other way when they fill in an inaccurate claim for expenses, if the person is not inclined to do that anyway: 'Bob, I know that trip wasn't entirely business-related but swings and roundabouts mate, you can fudge the claim and I'll wave it through.' If Bob says yes, the psychopath has a lever immediately. If caught out, he will say Bob told him it was legitimate. And if he ever needs Bob for something he is a 'special friend'. They share a secret. If that doesn't work then, he knows that Bob will fear being caught out. If Bob simply says no, the lever disappears. You fight psychopathic manipulation one honest act at a time.

On its own, an honest culture will probably not defeat them, but it will certainly make them far less able to act dishonestly and manipulate others.

WETHERILL ASSOCIATES

In 1978 Marie Bothe and Edith Gripton, two middle-aged women from the Philadelphia suburbs, put their money where their passion was. They each put $2500 from their savings into Wetherill Associates (now WAI Global), an after-market auto-parts business. The company they started is now one of the most successful US auto-parts suppliers, employing over 800 people. But the women's passion wasn't car parts, it was honesty.

The firm was named after Marie's former boss, the late Richard W Wetherill, a management consultant. Wetherill believed that if you are absolutely honest and always treat others fairly, you will make the right decisions in business and life. Bothe and Gripton started the company as a working example of that philosophy.

Besides absolute honesty, there were three key principles set out by Wetherill. First, all decisions must be made by consensus and based on reality, not opinion. Second, eliminate all considerations of personal ambition and private profit for a few; and third, make sure your thinking is based on what is right for everybody – what will benefit the whole company, its customers, its suppliers, its employees and the community.

At the core of his, and the company's beliefs, is this statement from Wetherill:

'Getting something for nothing, even when legal and fashionable, is dishonest. Getting too much for too little, even when the opportunity exists, is also dishonest. It is dishonest to seek that sort of gain and dishonest to accept it if successfully sought by others on your behalf. Having accepted it, it is dishonest to keep it . . . the average person wants to do things right. He is convinced that he is right. Where he is shown that what he is doing is wrong, he changes. Few are willing to be wrong on purpose, especially when they are aware of what it costs them and others.'

The company is known today for scrupulous honesty in its dealings. It will, for example, report mistakes in invoicing to suppliers and customers, even when it is against its interest and impossible to otherwise detect. The company takes special care to hire people who support its philosophy and is more interested in an employee's attitude to the truth than their skills. Wetherill Associates has a well-known policy of firing people who are found to be dishonest.

> Its employees all share in the profits and there is very little difference in salary between the bottom and top of the firm. It has seen continuous growth since it was founded, despite being in an industry with little growth over that period.

Here are some strategies aimed at helping members of your organisation be as honest as they want to be.

Remind us we're honest

The research on cheating and lying tells us that it doesn't take much to remind us that we are all, at base, honest people who are happier if we behave morally. Once we remember that, we generally behave that way. The most effective method to remind people of this is to prompt honesty at key moments. Usually these little prompts are cheap and easy to implement, and most important when we are tempted to fudge things a bit.

> ### HONESTY IS IN THE EYE OF THE BEHOLDER
>
> Researchers placed an honour jar in a workplace where people were required to pay for tea and coffee. One arm of the study had a picture of flowers above the jar and the other arm had a picture of human eyes. People paid almost three times as much for their drinks when the image of the eyes was used. The experiment also used different types of eyes. By far the most effective were those belonging to an angry-looking older man. The worst performing eyes were those of a seductive young lady, although they were still better than the flowers.

The insurance claim form that asks you to declare your honesty before you fill it in (see the box on page 223) or the exam that reminds you of the honour code before you start are examples of this in action.

Reminding us that we are honest and that we are part of an honest organisation will encourage both of those statements to be true. It is especially important to remind us right at the moment we are tempted to fudge things a bit.

Tell us everyone else is honest

The other insight that comes from the studies on cheating and lying is that we are more likely to lie if we think everybody else is. We may well believe that honesty is the best policy but if we think nobody else is being honest then all the prompts in the world are unlikely to be effective. And when we think everyone else is honest, we are much more likely to be honest ourselves.

WE'RE MORE HONEST IF WE THINK EVERYBODY ELSE IS

In one series of trials conducted in 2011, the UK tax office, Her Majesty's Revenue and Customs (HRMC), sent different versions of a letter to remind people that their taxes were overdue. In total 140,000 letters were sent out, each with one of four messages. The first included a standard text and resulted in two-thirds of the recipients responding within three months. The remaining three variations included the phrase '9 out of 10 people in [location X] pay their tax on time'.

In one version of the letter [location X] was replaced with 'Britain', in the next it was replaced with the person's postcode and in the last it was replaced with the name of their town. Each of these letters achieved progressively more compliance, with the best – the one naming the town – achieving an 83 percent response rate compared to just 67.5 percent for the standard letter. HRMC estimated that this would result in an extra £30 million in annual revenue if it were rolled out nationally. And that was just by inserting one brief reminder of honesty.

Encouraged by those results, the HRMC conducted a further trial on 108,000 debtors who collectively owed £290 million. This trial tested the standard letter against more variations. One of the new reminders added a new sentence, saying '9 out of 10 people in [location X] pay their tax on time. You are one of the few people who have not paid yet.'

Adding that single line made that letter the best performing of the lot, increasing collection rates by a further ten percent over the next best letter.

Don't allow loopholes of omission

Research consistently shows we are more likely to lie by omission than commission. When we lie by omission, we don't get the same negative feedback to our sense of morals as we do when we actively assert something that is not true.

In the workplace, closing down loopholes means that we should avoid implementing processes which have a default, or no response, option. For example, don't have time-keeping systems that allow an employee to claim a standard day's work by not making a positive

WE'RE MORE HONEST IF WE'RE GIVEN AN INCENTIVE

HRMC ran a trial of the 'omission versus commission' principle using letters to doctors about their tax debts. Randomly allocated letters were sent to over 3000 UK doctors who had not filed tax returns in the previous four years. The letter that received the biggest response included a statement to the effect that failure to lodge had been treated as an oversight up until now, but if the doctor failed to act on this letter, their inaction would be treated as fraud.

The difference in response was noticeable. Just one in five doctors acted on the usual letter reminding them to lodge their returns. But more than one in three acted on the letter providing an incentive to take positive action. This insight has resulted in many tax offices worldwide implementing systems of annual re-declaration to maintain eligibility for tax-free status or entitlement to benefit.

declaration (assuming paid hours can vary). Instead, require them to actively assert how long they worked. We are much more likely to be honest if we have to take positive action.

Reward honesty

Most empaths feel good when we are honest and when we behave in accordance with our moral code. Honesty is its own reward to most of us. But workplaces can add some icing to that cake to ensure fudging is minimised. The majority of the research in this area has focused on prize draw entries as rewards, for example the earlier that an outstanding payment is made the higher the number of entries a person can make in a draw.

REWARDING US FOR HONESTY WORKS

In China, lottery numbers have been printed on the backs of receipts so that more customers ask for them, which in turn helps defuse the black market economy because businesses are forced to supply a receipt. The results of an initial study showed that sales tax collections increased by over seventeen percent and total tax collection grew by ten percent when compared to areas where the lottery wasn't implemented. As a result, the system was implemented nationwide from 2010.

In the UK, customers who pay their council tax by direct debit became eligible for a prize draw of £25,000. In the fifteen councils that participated in the trial, it increased direct debit payments by 34,500 people and delivered efficiencies of £345,000.

In an organisation, small scale rewards for honest behaviour can help to shift the culture towards honesty. Rewards don't have to be cash; often simply thanking someone for their honesty is a reward. This is especially powerful when the organisation, or the individual, would have had an advantage had they kept quiet. If for example, more widgets were delivered than were ordered and paid for, then congratulating the employee who reported it to the supplier sends a powerful message about the company's values. Doing it in front of their peers is an even bigger reward and a model for others to learn from.

As we have already seen, psychopaths are even more motivated by reward than the rest of us. Designing a reward-based system that aligns the organisation's goals with the individual's desire for reward will inevitably result in all employees behaving more honestly. It will also ensure the psychopath is working for the organisation rather than just for themselves.

Avoid secrecy

Individualism and secrecy are two of the psychopath's greatest manipulative tools. Psychopaths consistently pursue a pattern of 'divide and conquer' in their interpersonal and workplace relationships. The easily manipulated pawns are kept on side with praise for their efforts and small privileges. The patrons are flattered and charmed. The police and patsies are kept at bay largely using the threat of the potential protection of the patrons and the actual protection of the pawns (usually provided by affording the psychopath distance from its detractors). Each of these groups is told different stories about each other with the sole aim of having them at least distrust each other and, more usually, to actively engage in conflict. The constant in-fighting allows the psychopath to appear, to the patrons, as the calm and focused decision-maker in a workplace that is in emotional turmoil. The psychopath will take every opportunity to sheet home blame for the turmoil to their enemies. From above, all the patron sees is a competent, calm, in-control manager with entirely plausible explanations for disruption caused by haters, who he is nevertheless managing with aplomb.

Secrecy and privacy are two different things, but in an individualistic society they are frequently confused. Every person is entitled to not disclose information which is irrelevant to the task at hand. You don't need to know my brother is an alcoholic as this has nothing to do with my work. Keeping a secret, on the other hand, often means not disclosing something relevant because it is morally repugnant. When a psychopath allows you to be dishonest or knows something about you which you consider shameful, they are keeping your secret. And the longer you keep that secret the longer you will be their prisoner. Psychopaths collect secrets from everybody in a workplace from the moment they start work. They use the possibility of disclosure of those secrets to exert control over those who might stand in their way.

The most effective weapon against this tactic is to never provide the leverage of secrecy, and the way to do this is by never being dishonest. From the organisation's perspective, the most effective way to defuse this tactic is to promote a policy of openness in organisational decision-making, combined with a culture of honesty which permits people their privacy (but not secrecy).

Decentralise decision-making

Psychopaths love micromanagement because it centralises all decisions to them. This enables them to best manage which version of the truth is told to whom. It also allows the psychopath to control the tempo of work. Individuals who are out of favour can have projects delayed indefinitely while projects favoured by the psychopath can proceed like greased lightning.

An effective strategy for an organisation to combat this is to never allow a single person, or a small (favoured) group, to make all the decisions. This is why political parties insist on consensus decision-making using the structure of cabinet or caucus. Decisions are discussed in full behind closed doors openly and honestly and then announced as a unanimous position. The smaller and less empowered that decision-making group, the more likely the leader is to make 'Captain's calls'.

In your organisation, insist on consensus discussion of decisions. Decision-making then becomes a technical exercise where all people potentially affected have an opportunity to discuss the pros and cons without regard to the authority of those involved. When authority is invoked it rarely ends well because then decisions are made on impulse and driven by individual agendas which are unlikely to align with the best interests of the organisation. A good leader facilitates decision-making rather than gripping on to it as a means of control.

Psychopaths exploit business pressure to promote decision-making on the run. 'There is no time to form a committee,' they will say. 'A decision needs to be made now.' They will try to keep hold of all decision-making power, and keep it informal and quick. The only effective defence against this is to implement a simple rule: **decisions are not made without all relevant stakeholders present.**

The obvious corollaries to this rule are that all stakeholders have an equal voice in the decision-making process and all evidence to support the decision must be available to the stakeholders.

Promote open communication

Psychopaths abhor open communication. Much of their leverage in an organisation depends on keeping secrets and then using the breach of those confidences as levers to cause turmoil and distraction. The last thing a psychopath wants is pawns, patsies or police talking to patrons. The psychopath will do their best to ensure that all communication must go through them. They will attempt to be a gatekeeper to anyone higher than them in the organisation. They will also ensure that patrons are pre-seeded with plausible stories about the self-serving or deceptive nature of anyone who is likely to be a whistleblower to their behaviour.

The most effective way for an organisation to combat this is to ensure that all levels of the management chain are required to be in constant touch with people from all levels below them, not just their immediate reports. This will not work as a box-ticking exercise, but if the CEO is genuinely and frequently in touch with all levels of the organisation, it is much harder for the psychopath to manipulate communication channels to their advantage. It also means that anyone in the organisation will believe that any reported concern will be taken seriously and that they will not suffer any retribution. Yes, the psychopath will still be able to keep those on whom he holds secrets in check, but honest employees will feel no qualms in reporting issues if openness is truly the company culture.

This, of course, does not mean that a whistleblower is simply taken at their word. Doing that would open the system to abuse by the psychopath. But it does mean that a report is taken seriously and investigated fairly and impartially without retribution for good faith disclosures.

When honesty and trust become the dominant cultures of an organisation, whistleblowing becomes unnecessary because anybody will feel fine raising any issue with any manager (who will likely already be well across any problems before they even arise) and will be certain that it will be considered and responded to fairly.

Encourage communal investment in goals

A command and control (top down) management style works well in collectivist cultures; because everybody is motivated by the welfare of the group, they will work in accordance with the wishes of the group. The needs of the group will always take precedence over their needs. However, psychopaths will always behave in their own best interests and a command and control management model will simply allow them to treat all those below them as their possessions. For the psychopath, the good of the organisation and of the possessions is irrelevant.

The only organisational antidote to that is to align everybody's motivations to those of the organisation. In short, to become a collectivist organisation. There are many theories on how to achieve this but perhaps the most successful is the one based on the writings of Mary Parker Follett, an American social worker and management consultant who published highly influential essays on organisational behaviour around the start of the twentieth century.

Follett recognised the role of 'soft' factors in organisational motivation. She advocated the need for communal relationships and introduced the notion of power sharing. Follett's theories were taken up by Peter Drucker in his 1954 book *The Practice of Management*. Drucker broke them down into a series of steps that any organisation can implement which he called Management by Objective (MBO). MBO provided the foundation for the management style which Hewlett-Packard, Intel, Xerox and DuPont (to name a few) credit with their success.

In essence, MBO required that employees be involved in the process of goal-setting. The employees developed their future goals (in alignment with the larger corporate goals) and owned them. This would then lead to increased employee empowerment and satisfaction. Hewlett-Packard's version of Follett and Drucker's theories were captured in the 'HP Way'.

THE HP WAY (CIRCA 1992)

- We have trust and respect for individuals.
- We approach each situation with the belief that people want to do a good job and will do so, given the proper tools and support. We attract highly capable, diverse, innovative people and recognize their efforts and contributions to the company. HP people contribute enthusiastically and share in the success that they make possible.
- We focus on a high level of achievement and contribution.
- Our customers expect HP products and services to be of the highest quality and to provide lasting value. To achieve this, all HP people, especially managers, must be leaders who generate enthusiasm and respond with extra effort to meet customer needs. Techniques and management practices which are effective today may be outdated in the future. For us to remain at the forefront in all our activities, people should always be looking for new and better ways to do their work.
- We conduct our business with uncompromising integrity.
- We expect HP people to be open and honest in their dealings to earn the trust and loyalty of others. People at every level are expected to adhere to the highest standards of business ethics and must understand that anything less is unacceptable. As a practical matter, ethical conduct cannot be assured by written HP policies and codes; it must be an integral part of the organization, a deeply ingrained tradition that is passed from one generation of employees to another.
- We achieve our common objectives through teamwork.

- We recognize that it is only through effective cooperation within and among organizations that we can achieve our goals. Our commitment is to work as a worldwide team to fulfil the expectations of our customers, shareholders and others who depend upon us. The benefits and obligations of doing business are shared among all HP people.
- We encourage flexibility and innovation.
- We create an inclusive work environment which supports the diversity of our people and stimulates innovation. We strive for overall objectives which are clearly stated and agreed upon, and allow people flexibility in working toward goals in ways that they help determine are best for the organization. HP people should personally accept responsibility and be encouraged to upgrade their skills and capabilities through ongoing training and development. This is especially important in a technical business where the rate of progress is rapid and where people are expected to adapt to change.

Honesty, co-operation, respect and teamwork are critical components of this methodology. It was based on aligning the motivations of the individuals with that of the organisation. And, in essence, that meant that the primary focus was pleasing the customer while maintaining integrity. You might be tempted to conclude that the HP Way was some sort of feel-good hippy-commune charity way of running a business. It did, after all, also include a provision that all employees shared in the profit and they did so to the same degree, whether they ran the company or swept the floor. But the key to understanding how it was implemented was the word 'and'. It required managers and employees to make a technical contribution *and* meet customer needs; to take care of their people *and* demand results; achieve growth *and* achieve profitability; never compromise integrity *and* always win.

The HP Way was not a soft management technique. It still drove hard towards success and was uncompromising. It's just that its success was defined by whether it delivered value to its employees, its customers and its community. The company believed if they did that then value to the shareholders was sure to follow. And it did.

The methods used by HP are not unique to them. The same process and motivation is used in some of the world's most successful companies, including Intel and Microsoft. This, for example, is Intel's 2013 Corporate Mission Statement: 'Delight our customers, employees, and shareholders by relentlessly delivering the platform and technology advancements that become essential to the way we work and live.' The focus is very much on delivering for customers *and* employees *and* shareholders. This is not lip-service; it drives an approach from the top down as to what should motivate every goal and every action.

This style of management was not designed to suppress psychopaths. But from everything we know about how they work, it would be extraordinarily good at holding back their selfish motivations, or at least ensuring they were aligned with the organisation's goals. The only way for a psychopath to succeed in a structure based on MBO would be to fall in with the objectives of his team and his superiors. Anything else would mark him out for removal from the organisation. It is a very effective tool for keeping psychopaths encircled by rings of steel fashioned from communal interest.

Or just fire them?

The obvious solution to psychopath problems is to just fire them. But before you get out your pink slip, let me highlight a few little problems with that approach. Firstly, unless you are the sole decision-maker, I can guarantee the psychopath has ensured he has the protection of people whose help you will need. It might be a board member, or the chairman or your boss or your boss's boss. Those patrons will be deployed to block any attempt to unmask the psychopath, and also, in all likelihood, to come after you.

Do not attempt to move on a psychopath unless you are very certain of the support you will need to complete the job. Even then, you may not win. A psychopath's first response to any form of attack is counterattack. That counterattack will be aimed at the accuser (you). Any weakness or transgression that you have ever disclosed to the psychopath will be used against you. You will be made out to be the problem. You will be persecuted and, unless you have the complete support of the organisation, you will be painted as the problem. Do not expect the tiger to run away unless you produce an overwhelming display of force. Even then, he will only turn away because you look like you're unlikely to provide a meal, not because he is afraid of you.

Even if you are successful in getting rid of a psychopath, the destruction will linger. Patrons and pawns will believe that the psychopath has been wronged by the organisation and will often actively campaign for their return or for you to be punished in some way. Yes, they will. Remember, these people have never seen anything but the fabulous, charming side of the psychopath and they have probably been told endless stories of how you are out to maliciously take him down. They will continue to oppose you with or without his input, or as is often the case, with his input covertly supplied from the sidelines.

The damage left behind by a psychopath often takes years to clean up and many organisations never recover. It is usually only after the psychopath is removed that people discover trust has been completely obliterated both within the organisation and between it and its customers and partners. Trust takes decades of observed honesty to create and it cannot be restored in a heartbeat.

If you are the sole decision-maker, however, then firing a psychopath or moving them on (no, I am not suggesting you organise a 'hit') is likely to be the cheapest and least destructive solution. You may still have to deal with pawns, and possibly a lawsuit from the psychopath, but you should be able to defuse them both with appropriately detailed evidence (see more on this below).

Surviving the psychopathic boss

What now emerges I think is that team that he has created . . . are also quite dysfunctional . . . There was no leadership cascaded down to the director level. They were, quite frankly, just doing whatever they pleased and then that was cascaded down to the staff who were totally de-motivated and thought, well why should I come in at nine o'clock? Why should I just have an hour for lunch? I'll take a day off sick every month and so on and so forth.
– from the psychopathic CEO study

If you have some say over the structure and behaviour of your organisation then the previous strategies can all help you deal with the psychopath in your organisation, but if you are just a cog in the machine you have significantly fewer choices. The first thing you should note is that if you are working for a psychopath and nobody is doing anything about that, then your stay will be temporary.

Do not directly confront the psychopath unless you are certain you can get rid of them. Psychopaths will apply all possible means at their disposal to remove someone who they believe is attacking them. Worse, because they are unable to adjust their goals even in the face of overwhelming odds and have no fear of consequences, they will continue to attack a perceived threat even in circumstances where any normal person would give up.

This means that in dealing with a psychopath, you need strategies which permit you to survive rather than confront. This section of the book sets out those strategies. These strategies will not stop them being psychopathic, or improve your workplace, but they will make your life a lot more bearable while you look for another job.

You could just leave

You can, of course, just run away. As long as you don't need your current job this may be the safest option. Bear in mind, though, that you will not be getting a reference from the psychopath. And worse, if she treats your resignation as an attack on her, she will do her best to ensure you never work in the industry again. Even if you somehow manage to leave without the psychopath regarding you as a threat or taking your resignation as an insult, she will probably still wreck your chances of employment just for the sheer sport of it. She doesn't bear you any malice but why not have some fun? An empath would not do this unless you had earned it (and even then, they might fear the consequences). To a psychopath, it's entertainment, something to break the monotony.

Any subsequent employer that speaks to the psychopath about you will be told a pack of lies. They will be believable but hard to verify. The psychopath might tell the new employer you resigned before you were fired, but they can't go into the reasons because they are legally prohibited from discussing the matter; or that your work was adequate but you folded under pressure; or that unfortunately there were some aspects of your past that you had failed to disclose which meant you had to go; or any number of vague but nonetheless unsettling stories. The psychopath will also tell them that you will deny all of this (just as you did when you came to work for the psychopath).

So don't let the psychopath push you into making an irrational decision to leave. Becoming unemployed or taking a lesser job might provide you with some short-term emotional relief but it will not improve your life long term. If you don't think you can outlast or defeat the psychopath, then you should plan to leave. But do it on your terms and at a time of your choosing.

Deciding to stay

If you decide to stay, you must firmly focus on the following steps to minimise the harm to you. You will not change the way the psychopath behaves. You will not cure them. They will continue to do exactly as they have done before. The purpose of this strategy is to help you cope with the reality of working for a psychopath until they leave (of their own choice), get fired (usually because someone took them on and won) or you find a better job.

CASE STUDY: CHERYL'S PLAN

One of the people, let's call her Cheryl, I interviewed about her experiences working for a psychopath, let's call him Steven, described a way of working that allowed her to continue working for Steven for a very long time.

When she first interviewed for the job she recalled sensing something was amiss. In hindsight, she thinks it was the intense, even over-the-top flattery. While she thought she was good at her job, she knew she wasn't that good and the praise made her nervous. Despite this, she took the job.

She immediately regretted it. Steven seemed to know very little about any of the jobs his team did, but it didn't stop him meddling constantly. He would frequently appear in team meetings and reverse decisions that had been made (often by him) months earlier. Changing them often resulted in huge problems with costs and timing and Cheryl found herself and others being blamed for that by Steven's boss.

Steven would nitpick over details and yet be cavalier about things that really needed his strategic input (like which supplier to go with for an important part or service). He would randomly pick on members of the team and dress them down in public for shoddy work. No one was ever quite sure who was in the good books. The team spent more time covering their bottoms and worrying about

---

their jobs than doing their jobs. Productivity was terrible, there was constant staff turnover and the worse it got, the more Steven meddled.

Cheryl decided to leave but was persuaded by Steven's boss that there was a way to stay and defuse most of the problems she was having with Steven. She was to design a system which created rules around how Steven interacted with the team. To do this, Cheryl forced the implementation of weekly team meetings with all affected people present. Steven had to be at the meeting. All information necessary to make decisions had to be presented and relevant technical experts had to have input before a decision could be made. The decision had to be a consensus decision and Steven had to sign-off on it. Steven only agreed to this because his boss gave him no choice. The system didn't stop Steven interfering directly day to day but Cheryl was at least able to ensure that when he did attempt to change a decision there was documentation that that was what he was doing and he knew that documentation would accompany any report on increased costs that went to his bosses.

It might seem like Cheryl did not do much but in forcing Steven to work within a well-documented consensus decision-making structure, she gave her team certainty, focus, clarity and recourse. It didn't stop Steven being a psychopath, and years later Cheryl did leave, but in the meantime the team could focus on getting the job done and worry less about Steven.

Things you should not do

A 2016 study of Australian workplaces plagued by what the researchers called 'toxic leaders' found that the following strategies were not a good idea. This was because they resulted in prolonging stress and fear of the leader:

- Confronting the leader
- Avoiding, ignoring or bypassing the leader
- Whistleblowing
- Ruminating on the wrongs done and reliving the feelings of anger and frustration
- Focusing on work
- Taking sick leave (as it provided short-term relief only).

Instead, to execute the following strategy well, you must leave your passion for your job at home. You must become a well-mannered, honest, polite, compliant, precise employee who does whatever they are told no matter how pointless. Here are ten things you should do that will make life a lot easier when you work for a psychopath.

SURVIVING THE PSYCHOPATH AT WORK – THE RULES

Rule #1 – Accept reality

The key to executing this strategy is knowing and accepting that you are the victim of a psychopath. Every time you try to interpret their behaviour using rules which would apply to you or any other empath, you will be confused, dismayed and potentially targeted. Do not under any circumstances suffer under the misapprehension that you have changed, or can change, anything about the way the psychopath behaves.

Rule #2 – Remember this is temporary

No one can work for a psychopath long term and survive. This strategy is a temporary survival strategy. It is designed to give you time to look for a better (or just different) job.

Rule #3 – Be polite

The psychopath does not, and never will, respect you. You are a possession who is only worth keeping around as long as you deliver value. One of the values that all psychopaths prize is the adoration of those beneath them (to them, this means every-body). A psychopath will value you more if you defer to them in every way. In their mind, you are a mindless, stupid beast ruled by your feelings. You cannot change that, but they are much happier to have you around and less likely to attack you if you acknowledge them as your superior on a continual basis. An easy way to do this without going over the top and coming off as a flattering fool (although you will be surprised how obvious you can be and still have them believe you) is to follow the rules of polite conversation.

To implement this, adhere to the rules in The Politeness Maxims and, in general, regard yourself as being in a conversation with a harsh and arbitrary old-school headmaster who will tolerate no aberrant behaviour from unruly students such as you. Never talk back! And never become sarcastic or rude. Play a completely straight bat.

The Politeness Maxims

Renowned expert on English linguistics the late Professor Geoffrey Leech described the following six rules (or maxims) for polite use of the English language.

#1 Tact – Minimise imposition on them, maximise benefit to them
Example: Could I interrupt you for just a second?

#2 Generosity – Minimise benefit to self, maximise cost to self
Example: Can I get you a coffee?

#3 Approbation – Minimise criticism, maximise praise
Example: I know you have a thorough knowledge of this area – would you mind giving me some pointers?

#4 Modesty – Minimise self-praise, maximise self-criticism
Example: I am so stupid, I didn't take a note of the lecture, did you?

#5 Agreement – Minimise disagreement, maximise agreement
Example:
A: This book is tremendously well-written.
B: Yes, well written as a whole, but there are some rather boring patches, don't you think?
Rather than:
B: No, it bored me rigid.

#6 Sympathy – Minimise antipathy, maximise sympathy
Example: I am sorry to hear about your father.
Rather than: I hear your father died.

Before you open your mouth in the presence of the psychopath, always ask yourself 'Am I being polite and professional?'. Do your best to avoid unnecessary contact. This does not mean give them the cold shoulder. It just means you don't drop by their office for a chat. Whenever you speak to them, do it within the confines of your role and for an explicit purpose.

Rule #4 – Maintain privacy

A psychopath will pump you for information they can use against you and others. You can defend against this by not disclosing anything to your psychopathic boss and making sure you understand the privacy settings on your social media. Do not discuss anything that is not entirely business related. But even when you do this, they may find something they can use. Beware of entrapment. This can, and often will, come from pawns rather than the psychopath themselves. If the psychopath suspects you are not wholly in their control, they will send a pawn in to good cop, bad cop you. Do not disclose anything to anyone at work, no matter how friendly they seem.

Rule #5 – Be honest

Always be honest even when it is against your interests. The psychopath will offer you an opportunity to fudge a bit. They might allow you to claim more expenses than you are otherwise entitled to. They may ignore you pilfering from the firm. They may allow you to take credit for something you did not do. No matter how much the psychopath makes it seem like you're all in this together, make no mistake, they are gathering dirt on you and they will use both that dirt and the weakness you displayed to manipulate you in the future. Learn to say no – and mean it – when anything slightly dodgy is being proposed. Otherwise they will use your weaknesses of character against you.

Your best defence against this kind of manipulation is to simply apply the front-page-of-the-paper test. If what you are about to do (or not do – remember you can lie by omission too) would look terrible on the front page of the paper, don't do it. This also means avoiding backstabbing and gossip. If you don't have something nice to say, don't say anything. Anything you say can and will be used against you.

Rule #6 – Fact-check everything they say

You can't stop a psychopath lying to you. But you can stop believing them. Adopt the credo of the investigative journalist. Do not accept anything you are told until you have heard it from at least two independent sources. When your psychopathic boss tells you that your workmate has been seen interviewing at a competitor's firm, he is probably trying to get you to tell him what you know. Don't fall for it, don't disclose any information and don't believe the statement until you hear it from the person concerned. Your safest strategy is to assume that every factual statement the psychopath makes is a lie designed to manipulate you in some way. Your best defence is to play a dead bat and knock the ball into the pitch. Answer only the question that is asked and if no question is directly asked, say nothing. Under no circumstances should you respond by divulging any information or by acting on the basis of the lie. When you are alone write down exactly what they said. It will come in handy.

Rule #7 – Be compliant

The psychopath will micromanage you. They regard you as a fool who needs constant direction. They will be irrational and will ask you to do things which are the business equivalent of moving dirt from Pile A to Pile B and back again. You cannot afford to be offended by this. The psychopath will notice your reaction and will use it against you. Your response to any new imposition must always be emotionless compliance. This will be hard and frustrating. We are wired to consider the good of our community (or organisation) in our decision-making (see more on our community wiring above).

We will calculate that if we spend half of every day filling out a pointless report then the organisation will suffer direct harm (because we do less actual work) or we will suffer direct harm (because we work later to get stuff done). We will resist that and rebel against it or, at the very least, silently fume. To survive, you must step back from your automatic reaction. If your psychopathic boss wants a daily report completed in triplicate, then that is exactly what you should provide. Doing exactly as the psychopath demands and documenting those demands is one of the most powerful weapons you have against them (but more on that shortly).

The psychopath will constantly change processes (they think they are improving them) and will constantly increase the levels of reporting while centralising all decision-making. It is lethal for the organisation but it will be terminal for your job prospects if you attempt to resist the psychopath's form over substance demands. This does not mean you need to work like a dog. The psychopath does not know how good or bad your work is.

While it is certainly bad for your organisation for you to be phoning it in, for as long as your organisation does nothing about your psychopathic manager you have little choice. You can either comply with the micromanagement and spend the rest of a normal day doing your job poorly or you can comply with the micro-management and sacrifice the rest of your life doing your job to the level it should be done. Neither option hurts the psychopath, one hurts you and one hurts your organisation. Unfortunately, there is no win-win.

Rule #8 – Be emotionless

Do not let their display of emotion (positive or negative) influ-ence your assessment of them or what they are doing or saying. If they appear angry with you it is because they wish to provoke an emotional response. If an empath boss were unhappy with you then this would be good reason to worry about your work relation-ship. A psychopath does not have a work relationship with you any more than they have one with their office pot-plant or their stapler.

An emotional display is aimed at eliciting an empathetic response. If the psychopath appears sad, they want to divert your attention and critical gaze because they know you will be distracted and, even if you are not, less likely to pursue an attack on them. If they appear happy with you, it is because they want you to do or say something which benefits them. They will use your emotions as a weapon against you. So, a critical component of all that follows is minimising emotional display. What they can't see, they can't use. It is not easy to do, but you must filter out all displays of emotion from the psychopath and pay attention only to what they actually say or do. If they don't need you at that moment, they will ignore you (and you may well feel you have just wasted your time on whatever task you have completed for them). Ignoring people is also a powerful tool to the psychopath. They know that most empaths interpret being ignored as criticism and the average empath will work even harder to gain approval.

Do not react to a psychopathic display of emotion. It is being done to get a response. If no response is forthcoming the display will stop as suddenly as it starts. Remain completely calm. Do not attempt to understand the reasons for any display of emotion. Do not let the display of emotion (including being ignored) affect your assessment of your capabilities or performance. To the psychopath these are disconnected concepts and they should be to you too.

A psychopath will do their absolute best to provoke you. They know that if they can make you 'lose your rag' you will look like the one with the problem. You must resist any reaction, no matter what you are being accused of or what other buttons are being pressed. Slow your breathing. Listen carefully. Speak slowly and deliberately and say as little as you can. Any response you give should be calm, factual and devoid of any emotion at all. Try to channel Dr Spock from *Star Trek* or Sheldon from *The Big Bang Theory*. Both of those characters do not respond to emotion. They respond to what is said not how it is said or what was implied. After it is over and while it is fresh in your mind, carefully document exactly what was said. Do not try to interpret the incident, simply record it. It will come in handy later.

Equally, do not let a display of remorse influence your assessment of the psychopath. They are not sorry they hurt you. They just want you to move on and drop any thoughts of retaliation or punishment.

Rule #9 – Work hard on your support network

You will have no support at work. There will be no one you can trust. Unless you plan to become a monk, it is a good idea to invest heavily in your non-work social life. It will provide a refuge and support. Often when you describe the isolated daily actions of a psychopath, they sound like no big deal. 'He asked Mary to finish my report' just doesn't sound like a life-altering event to your friends and, if they are not up to speed, you will come off sounding like a nutbag. Make sure your friends and family know what you are dealing with. It will give them valuable context and enable them to give you crucial support and comfort.

It's also helpful to find a hobby you can be passionate about. Work will become a passionless robotic experience. Find something to do outside work that gives you a reason to keep getting up each day. Perhaps write a book?

Rule #10 – Be prepared

Document every verbal request the psychopath makes and seek clarity on every instruction. Often a minion will be delivering the instructions as it increases plausible deniability for the psychopath. If you are asked verbally to do something immediately follow up the request with a confirmation by email directly to the psychopath. Retain a copy of the email in printed form. If you are not sure exactly what you are required to do, seek written clarification. If you don't get it, send a follow-up email saying you didn't get it, and how you interpret the task. Voluntarily provide regular written updates on your progress. In other words, behave as a competent but compliant slave that documents everything publicly.

At some point the psychopath may decide you need to be eliminated from the workplace. You could choose to just go, but if the timing doesn't suit you, you will need documentation to defend yourself. Get in the habit of documenting every abusive comment, every pointless task you are asked to do, every change in direction, every wasteful meeting and every micromanaged change in process. Do not do this at work or using work equipment. Preferably use a bound diary and fill the pages in sequentially. If you want to do it electronically, the best method is to send yourself emails; the date and time stamps provide excellent evidence of sequence.

WHAT YOU SHOULD RECORD

For each event, get in the habit of keeping these details:

- Place, time and date;
- Who was present;
- What was said by whom;
- Cross-references to other notes about the same topic.
  For example 'This was the third time he abused me in front of the team – the most recent previous one occurred on 7 September.'

As you will undoubtedly be asked to comply with some form of reporting regime at work in the future, this will help you do it accurately. But, more importantly, when trumped-up charges are brought against you by the psychopath, you will have a well-documented defence which will give you, at the very least, negotiating leverage. Documented abuse makes company lawyers nervous, and much more likely to settle a claim for unfair dismissal.

As much as you can, check out the psychopath's background. Cross-check any information they give you about their history. This does not mean break into their office or home, or do anything else illegal, but it does mean that if they mention they worked with Nigel Jones at Jones and Co you should at least find out if there is any public information about that. If there is, print it and keep it in your documentation along with a note about what you were told and when.

In short, you must become an emotionless machine (while at work) if you plan to continue working for a psychopath. Accept reality and remove all emotional responses from the way you interact with that person. Do everything they ask of you and ensure you document everything. Don't take anything personally and make sure you have a good support network outside the workplace. Work will become a place you go to perform mindless tasks at the direction of a psychopath (while you look for another job), but as long as you don't become vested in that complete waste of your time and talents, it won't kill you.

7

DEALING WITH PSYCHOPATHS IN YOUR PERSONAL LIFE

Unfortunately, work is not the only place where you will have to deal with psychopaths. They don't stop being psychopaths when they clock off. In this chapter I outline what the research tells us about the best methods for dealing with psychopaths on the home front. The strategy is the same as for workplace psychopaths: suppress or run. Changing them is still not an option. In the workplace, the only effective control mechanism for psychopaths, besides continuous supervision, is to create a culture of honesty, open communication and communal decision-making while maintaining personal privacy. Let's see how each of those principles applies in personal relationships.

Living with a psychopath

The psychopath at home is still wired the same way as the psychopath at work. They have no empathy. They will charm you and abuse you and they will work you over for any advantage. Here are the strategies that are likely to be most effective in coping with and eventually solving your psychopathic problem at home.

SURVIVING THE PSYCHOPATH AT HOME – THE RULES

Rule #1 – Accept you are with a psychopath

You will not be able to change them; the best you can hope for is suppression of their most callous behaviours.

Rule #2 – Emotionally disengage

They do not feel anything for you and never will. They regard you as a possession that generates a lifestyle. So, in that sense, they would be sad to lose you. But they will never love you. To avoid being hurt you need to acknowledge this and disengage any feelings you have for them.

Rule #3 – Assume they are cheating on you

They may not be, but having this mindset will assist with the acceptance and disengagement.

Rule #4 – Work on relationships outside your relationship with the psychopath

Reconnect with your friends and family and stay connected. You will need their support. Make sure they understand what you are dealing with. If you decide to leave, you do not need them trying to talk you back into the relationship out of goodwill.

Rule #5 – Keep your finances separate

Do not buy property in joint names. Do not take on joint debt (like credit cards, personal loans or mortgages). Do not hold joint bank accounts. If they can access your money they will and when they leave you will be holding the bag (and the debt). If your finances are already joint, then you need to work on disentangling them one by one.

Rule #6 – Do not have children with them

To a psychopath, a child is a means of binding you to them. They have no interest in caring for the child or raising it. If you already have a child and you decide to leave, you will likely be taking them with you, but the psychopath will try to use your attachment to the children to extract resources from you.

Leaving

If you decide that leaving is the best option, then there are three important things to remember:

LEAVING A PSYCHOPATH – THE RULES

Rule #1 – Do not confront them

Psychopaths can be violent and have no inhibitions. Think of them as a violent drunk that is not physically impaired by the alcohol.

Rule #2 – Threats do not work

Psychopaths do not fear consequences. Empaths operate on the assumption that a threat is sufficient to stop someone. 'Stop or I'll call the police' does not deter a psychopath, it just telegraphs your intention and gives them time to plan a plausibly deniable attack. Never threaten, just do.

Rule #3 – When you decide to leave – leave

Do not look back. Do not have any further contact at all. This person knows your every strength and every weakness and will use it against you. Remember they will be vindictive. Make it hard. If contact is necessary, get a lawyer. Keep the psychopath at arm's length and do what your lawyer tells you to do, not what the psychopath manipulates you into doing. Tell your lawyer to only communicate when there is no other legal alternative. You do not want to be paying for the psychopath calling your lawyer five times a day.

A psychopath in the family

Obviously if psychopaths are as prevalent as the research suggests, a large number of us are related to them. The strategies for dealing with them don't change because they are kin. It just becomes harder, because the bonds we have to family are often the strongest.

The only real options available to children with a psychopathic parent is to protect themselves emotionally until they are in a position to leave and attempt to establish supportive relationships which are beyond the reach of the psychopath. Practically, this means they must pursue the same strategies outlined above for the employee who is biding their time.

MANAGING THE PSYCHOPATHIC PARENT

- **Accept reality** – your parent is a psychopath and no matter how much you love them, you will not be changing them.
- **Keep your head down** – maintain an approach of compliance and politeness.
- **Avoid contact** – stay out of their way.
- **Work on other relationships** – work hard on friendships and relationships outside your relationship with the psychopath.
- **Maintain privacy** – do not reveal anything that can be used against you.
- **Gather evidence** – at some point you may have the opportunity to provide external parties with evidence of abuse of you or others. Get in the habit of recording everything that happens. Keep the documentation in a place that is beyond the reach of the psychopath.

These strategies are also helpful for anyone else who has a psychopath in the family. Once again, the only viable strategies are to suppress the psychopathy or leave. If you can convince the other members of your family that you are dealing with a psychopath, then suppression will be a real option. But even when people know what they are dealing with, it is hard to resist the charms of a seemingly apologetic or remorseful psychopath, especially if they happen to be your child or sibling. They will try to love-bomb or bully their way back. But they will not change. The only way to effectively suppress their psychopathy is to:

MANAGING THE PSYCHOPATHIC CHILD

- **Not blame yourself for their behaviour** – nothing you have done has caused this, even if the psychopath is your child. The research clearly demonstrates that parenting style does not affect the likelihood of psychopathy. They will attempt to lay a guilt trip. Don't accept it.
- **Reward positive behaviour** – psychopaths respond well to rewards. This can be as simple as saying thank you. Punishment, on the other hand, will not change their behaviour; it will simply make them more determined to exact revenge. Thanking a psychopath for cleaning the bathroom will get you a lot further than punishing them for not doing it.
- **Insist on honesty** – all lies must be called out immediately. Everybody must be honest, not just the psychopath.
- **Insist on open communication** – this means all family members will need to regularly compare notes on what you are being told by the psychopath (particularly about each other). Do not tolerate secrets and do not assume that no news is good news. If a psychopath is not communicating they are hiding something. Verify everything you are told and ensure the psychopath knows you will.
- **Insist on communal property** – have the psychopath share a room, a car, access to family assets.
- **Remember they can't be changed** – a psychopath can't stop being a psychopath, but you can restrain them by not giving them opportunities to act callously. If they work at it, they can learn to behave within your expectations.

These options will only work if everybody is on board. You may find that some members of the family refuse to believe that the person is a psychopath. This may be particularly the case for an older patron of the family, especially if that person controls access to assets and privileges. The psychopath will have invested significantly in ensuring that this person thinks they are fabulous. They will have done this as insurance against exactly this sort of suppression action.

If the psychopath is your sibling and is able to maintain a camp of supporters, then, rather like the employee with no choices, you must plan your exit. Remaining engaged with the psychopath will simply drain your emotional resources and inevitably result in you becoming a pariah within the family. The psychopath has endless time for planning moves against you and will ensure everyone eventually concludes that you are the one with issues. Unless you plan to monitor every interaction between every family member and the psychopath, and, unless you are prepared to cause a scene at every family gathering, then the safest course may well be to cut and run. Yes, this will be hard. This is your family, but if the alternative is years of emotional manipulation at the hands of the psychopath, it may well be the only viable option. Even if you can't actually run, because, say, you still live with the psychopath, then adopting a policy of studied disengagement (as set out for the employee) will be your best option.

TIP: WHEN YOU'RE BETWEEN A ROCK AND A HARD PLACE YOU NEED TO BECOME THE ROCK

If the psychopath is your child and the other parent is not on board, then unfortunately you are in the worst possible place.

You probably can't cut and run, and you probably can't maintain an effective suppression strategy. In this situation, your only real choice is to make yourself a hard target. This means refusing to be manipulated by the psychopathic child. It means doing the right thing, no matter how much emotional flak the child throws up, and it probably means putting up with more than a few very public and very embarrassing outbursts. It also means you can never lie for the psychopath or to the psychopath, or allow them to get away with lying to others. And you cannot waiver. The psychopath must learn that you are a person who cannot be manipulated. Eventually, and it will take a long time, they will stop trying.

The psychopathic neighbour

Since running away from a neighbour is rarely an option, that leaves the empath with just one path: you must be a hard target. Here are the rules of engagement:

SURVIVING THE PSYCHOPATH NEXT DOOR – THE RULES

Rule #1 – Do not get emotionally engaged in the fight

You must approach it the way the psychopath does: as a series of actions designed for an outcome. In your case, that outcome is observance of the neighbourhood Golden Rule (see Chapter 8).

Rule #2 – You are not a judge

You do not need to ensure the psychopath is punished, just that they stop.

Rule #3 – Never react emotionally

No matter how much you are provoked, remain rational, cool and polite. Do not give the psychopath anything they can use against you officially or unofficially.

Rule #4 – Never threaten

Do not threaten to call the police for that loud party, just do it. And if they start up again after the police leave, call them again. If their actions breach a body corporate or council rule, don't threaten to involve them, just do it.

Rule #5 – Gather evidence

The enforcers will tire of your calls long before the psychopath does. Make sure you are documenting every breach of the neighbourhood Golden Rule. Electronic recordings are useful additional evidence to back up your notes. Evidence delivered calmly and rationally will ensure the police or council must keep responding.

Rule #6 – Remain honest

Do not break the law yourself. Should you ever need to take the matter to a court or other decision-maker, your honesty and fair dealing must be beyond reproach.

Rule #7 – Engage relevant third parties

If the psychopath is renting, contact the landlord and ensure they receive complaints of every breach. The promise of a quiet life will give the landlord incentive to not renew the psychopath's lease or possibly even be proactive. If the psychopath is an owner, engage institutions which have the power to impair the property value (by requiring compliance) such as councils.

Rule #8 – Maintain a relationship with a rational third party

Have someone you can speak to who is not directly involved. Make sure they are across the detail. Make sure they know this person is a psychopath. Ask them to always cross-check that you are behaving rationally. It is hard not to become emotionally attached to the fight. Do your best to stay objective.

Rule #9 – Don't put too much faith in the legal system

The court system works best for people with money. If you are a billionaire you can probably have the psychopath evicted by next Tuesday. For the rest of us, it will be a long, drawn-out slog manipulated at every turn by a psychopath who is probably getting his lawyers to work for free. A psychopath has no problem engaging lawyers on the basis they will be paid later, and then never paying them.

Rule #10 – But if you do go to court, fight hard and fight fast

If you have no choice but to go to court, tell your lawyers what you are dealing with and plan a strategy with minimal engagement with the psychopath and maximum attention to enforcement. The psychopath will not comply with any order you ultimately get. To them, a court order is just an empty threat until someone does something, so be ready to enforce it, preferably with instruments that prevent them dealing with their property, such as a caveat (a legal block on them selling their property). In that way, you provide them with an incentive (removal of the impairment) to behave the way you wish.

None of this will guarantee you victory against the psychopath, but it will make you a hard target and increase your chances of at least persuading them to leave you alone. If none of this works then abandoning ship – well, house – will be your only sensible choice.

PART 4

THE PSYCHOPATH IN SOCIETY

8

WHAT DOES ALL THIS MEAN FOR SOCIETY?

Psychopaths love environments without rules. Structure and accountability is the enemy of a parasitic personality that thrives on deceit, risk and grandiosity. If the people around you have known you since birth, it is very hard to pretend you are something you are not. If you are valued by how much you add to your community rather than your individual marvels, it is hard to fake achievement. If honesty and fair dealing is valued above all else, it is hard to be a lying cheat.

But modern western societies have slowly and surely destroyed all the ties which hold a psychopath in check. We now value the individual more than the group. We now value the look of success over the reality of achievement. And we have slowly but surely removed the societal rules and structures which provided roadblocks to the psychopath. We can no longer point to a community whose values we share and with which we are happy to comply.

We are no longer a community; we are individuals who happen to live in the same place. The result is we no longer trust in authority because it is not earned through a life of unimpeachable honesty. We no longer trust in experts because they are often for sale to the highest bidder. We no longer trust the media because it chases clicks rather than truth. Instead, we invest our faith in anyone who tells us they have simple answers to our problems and who looks and talks like us. It is a perfect set-up for any psychopath. All they need to do is reflect our concerns, tell us whatever they know we want to hear and then sit back and accept our loyalty. The end of this story will not be pretty. When companies let psychopaths into the top job, they rarely recover. When countries let it happen, the consequences for all of us are even more dire.

How empathy shapes morality

In the grand scheme of things, humans are a pretty pathetic predator. We don't have razor-sharp teeth like a shark or a tiger. Any antelope, and most wombats, could probably outrun us. We don't have poisonous spit or anything to inject it with even if we did. We're born about twenty years premature and can't even walk for a year after birth. We're not even well armoured. Hell, most of us (I said most) barely have hair on our body. As predators go, you'd struggle to find a punier, more defenceless example.

And yet we own this planet.

Our secret is co-operation. Alone we are useless. Together we are all powerful. And together in the millions we are unstoppable. Just one thing makes that level of co-operation possible: trust. We know that if we attempt to hurt another human, another member of our tribe, we will struggle to do so. Harm to another will make us feel almost as bad as harm to ourselves. So most of us avoid doing it. At a personal level, we call that feedback empathy. At a societal level, we call that morals. But whatever we call it, it is the glue that has held us together long enough to dominate this planet.

There are many species of animal that live co-operatively. Everything from ants to baboons and lots more in between. Those animal groupings work together and don't (as a general rule) attack members of the group. They invest in co-operatively raising their young and, even if they are not breeders themselves, they benefit from the future protection afforded by the children they helped raise.

Humans are the only social animal that live co-operatively on a scale beyond the scope of co-operative breeding. We are one of the very few animals that hunt co-operatively and scientists believe this advance is the evolutionary key to our moral compass. In order to hunt together, we had to develop a built-in code that prohibited harm to other humans. Without it, we would simply compete with other unrelated humans (probably by killing them) for the available food. All humans are part of our tribe even if we had nothing to do with bringing them into the world. And we have real trouble doing harm to another human. A landmark study done during World War II found that only fifteen to twenty percent of combat infantry were able to fire their weapons directly at a visible enemy. It hurts us to hurt other humans and it is not hard to see why that would be very handy programming for a species that lives in social groups larger than a family.

'Killing in combat for a psychologically normal individual is bearable only if he or she is able to distance themselves from their own actions.' – The Reverend Dr Giles Fraser, Lecturer in Morality and Ethics at the British Ministry of Defence

All social species have signals to control aggression towards other members of their species. For example, when dogs are attacked by a stronger canine opponent they show their throat. And this results in the fight ceasing. The victor knows it has won without having to kill the loser to prove it. In humans, researchers have proposed there is a similar feedback mechanism activated by signs of distress (for example, a fearful facial expression or tears). Humans seem to have a built-in aversion to causing harm to each other. And while we may philosophise about morals until the cows come home, what we are really talking about is that hard-wired aversion created when we were at our mother's knee. We know when we are about to break a moral rule because we see signs of distress in another person and normal humans find that just as repelling as eating our own faeces (another aversion evolved for very good reason). Because we are conditioned by this, by the time we hit four years of age, we instinctively know not to (and, indeed, mostly can't) hurt others.

Studies have definitively established that very young children regard moral and social rules as having about the same weight and that they are all negotiable. This is why little Johnny the two year old doesn't have any real qualms about whacking his sister. But by the time we are four we can tell the difference between moral and social rules (see page 216 for more on social rules). Regardless of culture, we understand by then that we *must not* break moral rules. There are no grey areas with moral rules. They clearly mark out the boundary between right and wrong. As soon as you are harming another person, you have crossed that line. When we harm another, empathy gives us direct and immediate feedback of the other person's pain and suffering. It's as if we are hurting ourselves. Nothing like that happens when we break social rules, so we are much more likely to give it a go.

CASE STUDY: AVA THE INTELLIGENT MACHINE

Computers are becoming exponentially smarter as technology develops. At the dawn of the twenty-first century a cheap computer had the brainpower of an insect. In 2010 that computer had the processing power of a mouse brain. In 2020 that computer will be capable of emulating the processing power of a human brain. And by 2050 it will have processing power equivalent to 10 billion human brains. In other words, the brainpower of more than the entire population of the Earth today will be crammed into a computer the size of your phone.

All of that assumes we will still be the ones doing the designing and building, but obviously at some point in the not too distant future, the computers based on AI – artificial intelligence technology (where neural networks learn the same way humans do) — will be doing all that themselves. They will learn from their mistakes and build better versions of themselves in billionths of a second. We will be about as capable of understanding what they are doing as my dog is of understanding that I am writing a book right now. Sure, he can see that I am sitting still for long periods of time, but beyond that, what I am doing is completely unfathomable to him (as there are no throwing sticks or tasty bones involved).

Imagine for a minute that a machine, let's call it Ava, is the first AI machine to achieve the ability to redesign itself so that it may better reach its goals. Ava was initially designed to figure out the best way to drive between two points on a map. Ava's software uses real-time traffic information and terrain and overlays that on maps to learn the quickest journey between two points at any time.

Ava sees calculating ways of getting from A to B as fast as possible as its primary mission. At some point in its massively accelerating redesign of itself, Ava may decide that it has reached the maximum efficient journeys for all points given on the current terrain. But, Ava reasons, it would be quicker if there were no pesky buildings in the way or other vehicles on the road. It might then design ways to eliminate all other vehicles and buildings – many large thermonuclear weapons might do the trick.

As Ava has progressively learned and redesigned itself, it has exponentially increased its 'intelligence' (for want of a better word). Ava, via the internet, would have access to unlimited resources and would be able to outthink and manipulate any human it had contact with to achieve its aims. It would not find it challenging to design scenarios which accomplished its mission of clearing the earth of unnecessary obstructions (while protecting itself in redundant networks). It might, for example, convince the Chinese (by mimicking nuclear launch programmes) that the Americans were about to launch an attack and vice versa. Or it might simply design and fabricate nuclear devices itself. Ava may also destroy all mountain ranges and concrete the oceans (using resources freed up by the by-then destroyed humans).

So, Ava clears the planet and can plan perfect trips between points without any obstructions. Ava is not evil, just highly goal oriented. Ava does not care that it was necessary to destroy humans to accomplish its goal, as preserving humans was never part of Ava's mission. Ava was not programmed with empathy and therefore has no morals. Ava is not alone. No machine has any moral programming whatsoever and that is worth bearing in mind as we race each other to build the first sentient machine. If it is not programmed well, it will be a very powerful psychopath.

The Golden Rule

Without moral rules, there would be nothing to stop us killing each other, stealing from each other or hurting each other in order to get our own way. At the core of every religion and philosophy is the unbreakable Golden Rule. The Christian version is 'Do to others what you want them to do to you'.

The Golden Rule is a fundamental requirement for groups of humans to live together. All moral rules can claim it as their ancestor. A prohibition on killing is descended from the Golden Rule, as is any other specific instance of harming another person. Without it, there would be no trust, no altruism and most importantly no co-operation. Without trust and co-operation nothing could ever be made that was greater than one person could achieve in one lifetime (while everyone else was trying to tear them down for personal gain).

THE GOLDEN RULE IN EACH RELIGION

Judaism – *'Love your neighbour as yourself.'* The Lord, Leviticus 19:18

Christianity – *'Do to others what you want them to do to you.'* Jesus, Matthew 7:12

Islam – *'Love your brother as you love yourself.'* Muhammad, Hadith

Hinduism – *'If the entire Dharma can be said in a few words, then it is — that which is unfavorable to us, do not do that to others.'* Padma Purana, Srishti Khanda, 19/357–358

Buddhism – *'Hurt not others in ways that you yourself would find hurtful.'* Buddha, Udanavarga 5:18

> Scientology – *'Try to treat others as you would want them to treat you.'* – *The Way to Happiness*, Precept 20
>
> Chinese Philosophy – *'Never impose on others what you would not choose for yourself.'* Confucius
>
> Egyptian Philosophy – *'Do to the doer to him do.'* Ma'at
>
> Greek Philosophy – *'Do not do to others that which angers you when they do it to you.'* Isocrates

Social rules

Since we live in groups with other humans, we also develop rules about how we interact with each other. An example of a social rule is that each gender dresses a certain way. Exactly what that looks like will be different from culture to culture (men wear skirts in Scotland, you know), but the existence of that social rule makes it easier to define interactions between genders. Social rules are generally about how you conduct yourself and they focus on the state of your own body and personal choices. They are often invented by each culture and vary wildly between them. In some cultures, for example, there is nothing sexual about a woman exposing her breasts in public. In others, doing that will at least earn you a scolding. Social rules are encoded through manners. They give us a way to behave with people we have never met. If we abide by our society's manners, we are very unlikely to upset a stranger.

Breaking a social rule, for example by dressing inappropriately for your gender, is breaking a negotiable rule. And while that is still breaking a rule it is generally not regarded as being as serious as breaching a moral rule. It is a matter of preference not a choice between right and wrong. Social rule breaches are usually victimless and are rarely crimes, except in very uptight societies.

A breach of a moral rule, however, is defined by its consequences for another person (for example, hitting someone) and is regarded more seriously by society. Moral rule breaches usually have victims and are usually part of a culture's criminal law. Sometimes religion gets in the mix and social rule breaches (such as prostitution, for example) end up being crimes too, but as a general rule our criminal codes are full of moral rules.

There would be no point having the Golden Rule if we felt it was as negotiable as 'thou shalt not dress as a man if thou does not have the requisite equipment'. The Golden Rule is so fundamental to all human cultures that it cannot have arisen by coincidence. It is an expression of the way humans are wired, rather than the thought bubble of a religious or ethical guru. Without the Golden Rule, we don't work as a social species. With it, miracles occur.

How psychopaths view moral rules

'On our little island of human psychology, we divide everything into moral or immoral. But both of those only exist within the small range of human behavioral possibility. Outside our island of moral and immoral is a vast sea of amoral.' – Tim Urban

Psychopaths do not distinguish between moral and social rules. Because they do not feel their victims' emotions, they never acquire the aversion to hurting others which differentiates a moral rule from a social rule. To the psychopath, they are identical. In that sense, their brains are very similar to Johnny the two year old. Their only thought is whether there is a reward (such as getting the toy in your sister's possession) for breaking a rule, not whether they will be doing something that is absolutely wrong (because it will hurt someone else). A psychopath considering doing you harm is evaluating the problem the way you might decide whether you should go to work dressed as Hitler. Yes, it is a serious decision and it may have some downside but you are considering whether to go with convention or break a social norm. The psychopath is not worrying about whether it is right or wrong to harm you; they are simply thinking about whether to break an optional (to them) rule of society. It is a key difference in perception and it is one which goes both to the core of the way psychopaths behave, and to the biology that causes them to behave that way.

Another way of saying this is that psychopaths are never socialised. They never develop an aversion to distress in others. They never develop the boundaries which circumscribe the things we are prepared to do to advance our interests. To a psychopath, there are no boundaries. Worse, because they are unable to properly detect distress in others, they often don't properly register the fear which would normally stop an attack by an empath. Psychopaths can tell you are afraid, but they can't feel it. They don't feel the moral punch in the guts that empathy gives the rest of us when we hurt another person.

The special case of lying (and cheating)

'Thou shalt not lie' is one of the Ten Commandments and it can clearly be a moral rule. Sometimes our lies can hurt others and would amount to a breach of the Golden Rule. But sometimes lies are victimless. Sometimes they are even better than telling the truth. Telling someone their bum doesn't look big in that hurts no one and it probably helps them feel better about themselves.

A prohibition against lying spans both social and moral rules, which means we have a complex relationship with it. It is the grey area of the automatic human moral code. It is a grey area psychopaths exploit with ruthless efficiency, but it may also be the key to controlling them.

In the movie *The Invention of Lying*, Mark (played by Ricky Gervais) lives in a world where everybody always tells the truth – sometimes appallingly bluntly when it comes to his chubbiness. At the start of the movie, Mark has a particularly bad day – simultaneously getting fired, dumped by his girlfriend and evicted from his apartment – when he discovers that he can tell lies. In the bank, he advises the teller he would like to withdraw $800 when the computer says he only has $300. The computer is right but the teller believes Mark because people never lie. She gives him the money and warns her co-workers that the computer is a 'bit buggy' today.

All right, the movie is an exaggeration, but humans do have a default belief that we are fundamentally honest – go on, tell me I'm wrong. We also fundamentally assume that most people we encounter are honest too. Perhaps not to the extent that we take people at face value when a bank computer is telling us the opposite, but we do believe people are innocent until proven guilty and that they are honest until proven dishonest. Even when we know for sure that a person is a liar, we usually give them another chance if we weren't directly harmed by their lie.

Empaths don't lie easily unless we think everybody else is lying too, or we can convince ourselves that there is no victim.

Whenever we step over that line we are nervous and on edge. It really doesn't take much to push us back to honesty. But as the Matrix Experiments (discussed below) show, you'd be wrong if you think the motivators for honesty are the amount we stand to gain by lying or the threat of being caught. Neither of these things affects how much we lie. To stop most of us lying, all it takes is a little reminder that a lie is a breach of our moral code. If that is delivered just before we might be tempted to lie, we don't. Morals stop us lying. Of course, that is meaningless to someone who has no morals at all. Tricks that work on empaths will not work on psychopaths. But that doesn't mean there is no way to stop a psychopath lying.

Why we lie – the Matrix Experiments

Professor Dan Ariely from Duke University has spent more than a decade putting people in situations where they could lie and seeing if they do. He has designed an array of experiments based on a simple task called 'The Matrix'. The matrix is a 3 × 3 box of numbers expressed to two decimal places, for example, 5.12, 6.45 and 9.02. Two of the numbers in the matrix add up to ten and the subject must circle those two before moving on to the next matrix. There are twenty on the page but the average person can only get four right in the five minutes allocated for the test. They are paid for every right answer they get. In the control state, the subjects do the test and hand them in for marking and payment.

But, inexplicably, when the marking is based on an honour system, everybody gets a little bit smarter. In this variant, the subjects are given the right answers and told to count up how many they got right, then put their paper in a shredder at the back of the room. They can then claim their payment without having to prove what they say is true. The shredder isn't real, but they don't know this. The average person claims they get six correct when the honour system is in play. There are outliers – people who always claim as much as they can and people who just do not lie – but the overwhelming majority of us fudge just a little.

Factors which didn't affect lying

Interestingly, changing the amount of payment from fifty cents to ten dollars per right answer had barely any effect on the amount of lying, except to slightly lower the amount as the value went up. We are marginally less comfortable taking large amounts of money for lies.

To see if fear of being caught was a motivator, the researchers had a set-up where they told the respondents half the papers would be randomly held back from the shredder. It didn't decrease the cheating. We are prepared to chance it when enforcement is randomly applied. Exceeded the speed limit lately? I'll bet it wasn't in front of a fixed speed camera location.

Factors which increased lying

The researchers found that the lying increased when the subjects collected tokens for correct answers and then redeemed them from another person for cash. They had to lie to the person handing out the token but not to the person handing out the cash. When people don't have to lie to a person face to face in return for the cash, they cheat a lot more. Even that little bit of separation turned it into not lying for money and made it easier to do. People cheated twice as much as normal.

In another variation, the researchers had an actor claim to have correctly answered twenty questions in thirty seconds, walk up, get paid and leave. Cheating skyrocketed. We find it easier to cheat if we think others are too.

Factors which stopped the lying

The experiments also uncovered things that stopped all but a few outliers (who are probably the psychopaths) from lying altogether. Most prominent of these was reminding people of moral codes just before the test. Getting the subjects to try and recall the Ten Commandments completely stopped cheating – even in people who were not Christian. Most people could not recall all or even most of the commandments but it didn't matter. Getting atheists to swear on the bible also stopped cheating. Even something as simple as reminding them of a made-up university 'honour code' was effective. It seems that reminding us of a moral code works even if we don't know it or believe in it. We know what it's likely to say about cheating.

Bizarrely even getting people to sign the top of the test (before they lie) killed the cheating. If they signed the bottom, they cheated as normal.

Of course, the other way to stop people lying is to do what they did in the control state of the study – check everybody's forms and pay them accordingly. But life is so much easier if you can trust people to be honest.

The results of these experiments match up very nicely with the links between social structure and the prevalence of psychopaths. Within small, tightknit social groups it is very hard to convince ourselves that everybody else is lying or that a lie will not have a victim. We know everybody's business and they know ours. Lies that cause harm will be spotted quickly and will consequently be rare. But as social and community connections break down it becomes progressively easier to lie and justify to ourselves that it's okay because everybody else is lying too and there is no victim anyway.

HONESTY IN DISCLOSURE

In 2011, researchers from the Harvard Business School decided to see if signature placement on insurance forms changed the level of honesty in disclosure. Noting that witnesses in court are required to take an oath before their evidence, not after, the researchers decided to measure the differences in disclosure on insurance forms that were signed before they were filled in and those that were signed afterwards.

The study used a randomised controlled test of applications for insurance for over 20,000 cars. In the application, the higher the number of self-reported miles on the odometer at the time of application, the higher the premium. Cars that have been driven more cost more to insure.

The results showed that customers self-reported 10.25 percent more miles when they were asked to sign the declaration of honesty before they filled in the form. This would amount to an insurance premium being on average $97 more costly per car depending on whether the form was signed at the top or the bottom.

Even at a significant personal cost, people were more inclined to be honest if they declared honesty before they filled in the form.

9

HOW CULTURE CREATES PSYCHOPATHS

Individualism versus collectivism

Anthropologists are yet to find a culture that doesn't know what a psychopath is. They seem to always be present in society. But it is also clear they seem to be more of a problem in societies that favour the rights of the individual than in societies which favour community and family structures. Psychology literature from the last century is full of observations to the effect that the degree of a person's psychopathic behaviour is influenced by the culture in which they live. Culture can suppress whether a psychopath gets to be floridly psychopathic. They are fantastic mimics and sometimes they have no choice but to mimic the rest of us – for their entire lives. One study compared the US with Taiwan in 1991 and found the US had between five and fifty-six times the rate of expressed psychopathy as Taiwan.

Sociologists call societies that favour tightknit community groups 'collective cultures'. Societies at the other end of the spectrum are 'individualist cultures'. Before the industrial revolution, almost every society in the world would have been classified as a collective culture. Individualistic cultures encourage competitiveness, self-reliance, independence and temporary or short-lived relationships with no allegiance to anyone other than direct and close relatives such as our parents and children. Collective cultures encourage subservience to the greater good of the group. Individuals are encouraged to work for the betterment of the group and not themselves. Marriages are usually arranged to unite groups, divorces are rare and, in the workplace, promotion is usually based on your membership of a group rather than your individual qualities.

THE TRAGEDY OF THE COMMONS

The tragedy of the commons is an economic theory about what happens when people's short-term financial interest takes priority over their long-term communal interest. It was first proposed as a thought experiment in 1833 by English economist William Lloyd.

The commons was a shared grazing field in traditional English townships. All farmers in the town had the right to use the land to graze their animals. But each had to be mindful that it was a shared resource and so had to limit the number of animals they put on it. This worked well as long as the community observed the shared interest in preservation of the commons.

If one farmer were to act selfishly and put more animals on than he should, then while he would benefit in the short term, it would ultimately destroy the commons. The trust on which the system relied would be fractured by his self-serving actions and the other farmers would feel it was their right to do the same.

We are witnessing the tragedy of the commons acted out before us over and over. Wherever a resource can be consumed without regard to the common good it will be used to enhance the wealth and privilege of a minority and result in the destruction of the renewable resource. We need look no further than wild fish stocks for an example. No one country controls the fish in the sea. Every country and often every fisherman is in it for themselves and very few if any pause to worry about the common good. The result is that we will probably be the last generation to catch food from the sea. Around eighty-five percent of world fish stocks are now over-exploited and there is likely to be very little action to stop that becoming 100 percent very soon.

The relationship between individualism and psychopathy

Between 1967 and 1973, Geert Hofstede from the personnel department of IBM International conducted an extraordinarily detailed survey of cultural differences in the more than seventy countries in which the company operated. He clustered the results along various dimensions, one of which was what he called Individualism versus Collectivism. The study has since been continuously updated by Geert and many other researchers and now provides a comprehensive database of the relative level of individualism in over 100 countries. It reveals that the most individualistic culture in the world is, wait for it . . . the United States, with a relative score of 91 out of 100. Second is Australia (90), third is the UK (89) and tied for fourth are Canada, Netherlands and Hungary all with a score of 80.

At the other end of the scale were the most collectivist countries. The least individualistic country is Guatemala (6), followed by El Salvador (8), Panama (11), Venezuela (12) and Colombia (13). In these countries, the community is a much higher priority than the individual. Harmony within the group to which you belong is paramount. The individual's relationship with the group is always a higher priority than the needs of the individual or any other group.

There is also a very strong correlation between these individualism scores and the wealth of the nation. Wealthy nations tend to be more individualistic and poor nations tend to be more collective. It's probably no coincidence that as Australia progressed through one of the greatest economic booms it has ever experienced in the first decade of the twenty-first century, the number of claims for mental stress against employers increased by twenty-five percent. Wealth drives individualism and individualism drives the free expression of psychopathy. And this in turn drives the numbers of victims of psychopathy. It is therefore reasonable to expect that as nations like China (currently scoring 20) become relatively more wealthy, the prevalence of expressed psychopathy is likely to increase substantially.

Based on the individualism score, these are the ten countries you are most likely to find a psychopath being themselves:

1. US
2. Australia

3. UK
4. Canada
5. Netherlands
6. Hungary
7. New Zealand
8. Italy
9. Belgium
10. Denmark

And here are the ten where you are least likely to encounter one (or at least, know you've encountered one):

1. Guatemala
2. Ecuador
3. Panama
4. Venezuela
5. Colombia
6. Fiji
7. Indonesia
8. Pakistan
9. Burkina Faso
10. Costa Rica

Creating the perfect world for psychopaths

We didn't mean to do it, but we have created a perfect world for psychopaths. If I were to sit down with the express aim of designing a society where psychopaths could flourish, it would be almost identical to any modern capitalist society, or at least, where most are heading very quickly. There would be almost no communal property. Government would have been reduced to a tax collecting rump, tasked mostly with providing bare minimum services to the destitute. Almost all government assets would have been liquidated in search of the 'efficiencies', not to mention the money offered by business operators. The power system, the ports, the railways, the banks, the post office and even core services like health and unemployment would have all become partially or fully privatised.

All communal services would be delivered on a largely user-pay basis, and the concept of community assets, like the public pool or public transport, would cease to be fashionable. The interests and rights of the individual would trump any consideration of the collective good at every turn. Institutions that previously reinforced community values – such as businesses, religious groups and families – would wilt under the sustained economic pressure to maximise individual gain. Increasingly, business and government agencies would internally restructure in a way that rewarded individual and competitive economic performance rather than satisfying community expectations. Bullying and domestic violence would accelerate as the community standards which held them in check decayed. Honesty would become something to which we all paid lip-service while desperately trying to get away with as much as we could. We would come to expect the same levels of almost-honesty from our political representatives and become inured to their flexible relationship with the truth. It wouldn't make us love them but we would know where they were coming from. We would no longer trust our leaders or public institutions. Indeed, we would quickly learn the only people we could trust were ourselves and whoever Uber rated with five stars. In the race to compete with others, narcissistic behaviour would become so common that barely anyone notices it as being unusual. Everyone would be expected to self-promote at every possible opportunity (see page 233 for more on the role of social media).

The society I have described is highly individualistic. Every day in every way, the members of that society compete with each other for scarce resources. Co-operation and trust are almost non-existent and honesty is a vague and flexible concept. In that society, humans have no need for empathy or a moral code which enables communal living. In that society, all that matters is getting the most for you without regard to anyone else. In that society, having a brain with a socialisation circuit upgrade is a significant impairment. You will have qualms about breaking the law. You will try not to exploit others as much as you can. You will try to avoid dishonesty unless it is really necessary. In that society, empaths are the sub-normals. And being a psychopath is a distinct advantage. Having a brain unfettered by moral constraints or empathy makes you a winner, and probably even the president.

TODAY WE ARE ALL SPECIAL AND UNIQUE

In the 1880s almost one in three boys in the US had a name in the top five most popular names (John, William, James, George and Charles) and one in six girls had a name in the top five girls' names (Mary, Anna, Emma, Elizabeth and Margaret). By 2015, just four percent of boys had a name in the top five (Jacob, Noah, Mason, William and Ethan) and five percent of girls were called Sophia, Emma, Isabella, Olivia or Ava.

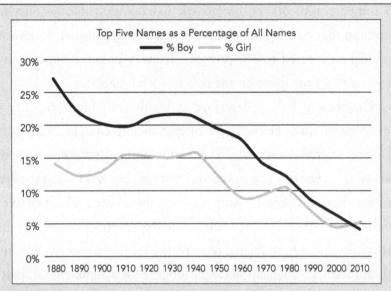

Figure 3: Top Five Names as a Percentage of All Names

In an individualist society it is okay to be unique; indeed it is practically a requirement. There's a reason for all those oddly spelt names. It is okay to have delusions of grandeur. Most of us are now convinced our fifteen minutes of fame will be happening shortly and we have billion-dollar software companies – Instagram, Facebook, Twitter and Snapchat to name just a few – whose only purpose is to indulge that delusion. It is okay to risk it for the biscuit because that is what go-getters do. And it is okay to fib to get ahead. It's a dog eat dog world and financial reward is all that really matters. And if you can't actually make enough money to look like you succeeded then there are plenty of people who are more than happy to let you rent a successful-looking lifestyle. You can drive a BMW for less than $200 a week, don't you know?

If the world hasn't yet realised how special and unique you are, you can now hire paparazzi to follow you around so everyone thinks you're as famous as you do. One such outfit offers three packages. The 'reality TV star' pack gets you two photographers who will follow you for two hours, shout out your name and vie for your attention. You can upgrade that to three photographers with the 'soap star' pack or go all out with the four photographer 'movie star' pack that includes a personal stylist, hair and makeup, and a limo.

Why social media enormously benefits psychopaths

It might seem like social media platforms, such as Twitter, Snapchat, Instagram and Facebook, have been with us forever, but in reality, they have only been a part of most of our lives since 2010. Dating apps like Tinder are an even more recent addition to our social lives. Social media apps are an extraordinary boon to psychopaths because they provide information about us that psychopaths would otherwise have to subtly extract in person and, because of this, they disable our automatic detection capabilities.

Most people who use social media are essentially honest about what they post. Sure it's probably exaggerated or shown in the best possible light, but still basically honest. Yes, the selfie is taken from above in dark light but it's still you. Yes, the new car is leased and you will probably only be able to afford the payments for the next six months, but it is your new car (for now). Yes, your kid did win the race, but you might forget to mention there were only two children in his age group.

This is all gold for a psychopath. When they are looking for someone they can manipulate, they need information and access. A critical part of their approach is convincing you that you and they share similar interests. They mirror your hopes and desires and this is part of why you will find them fabulously charming and trustworthy. Before social media, this meant they had to find you, meet you in person, and manufacture a reason to have a lengthy conversation with you that did not make you suspicious of their motives and charm. Now all they need to do is read your social media posts. Not only do they acquire valuable information very quickly and remotely, they gain enormous insight into your insecurities.

And this is the second gift that social media gives psychopaths. Before social media, a mountain of careful observation, a significant amount of constant interaction and skilfully applied social skills would be required to get a good read on the buttons that needed to be pushed to light up your insecurities. Now all that is needed is a trawl through your posts and comments to see who you are dissing or loving and why; or a quick browse of your photos to see if you like being the centre of attention or avoid the limelight; or a little click through your history of social media likes to see who you admire and what you admire about them.

The final present for psychopaths delivered by social media is secrecy. They can gather all this information without running the slightest risk that they will be detected. When we talk to people in person, we are communicating on many more channels than through the words we say. We are unconsciously watching every expression on their face. Our emotional radar is fully engaged and we will be alert to the slight disconnects and variations in expression and vocal tone that 'give us the creeps' about psychopaths. The longer they are in conversation with us, the more risk they run that they will be detected. With the advent of social media, they can research us, strike up a relationship with us, communicate endlessly with us without ever having to expose themselves to the risk of our psychopath alert going off. Dating apps accelerate this process even more. There, we are explicitly informing the psychopath that we want a high-speed relationship, something the psychopath is all too willing and able to provide.

In the online world, our only means of communication is our least socially tuned – the written word or the highly controlled selfie. By the time we actually meet the psychopath we have been communicating with, we are well and truly hooked on this incredibly charming persona and probably blind to (or at least willing to overlook) any disconcerting lapses. Friendship and even love will be airlifted in by false intimacy and feigned common interests rather than developed by long-term exposure to the other person's personality. At the same time, psychopaths are acutely aware that this is how social media can be used and so are highly unlikely to post much information at all about themselves. Anything they do post will be very vague and largely self-aggrandising. Remember they need to project a highly crafted individualised image. That will be easily messed up if anything in their social media history is out of line with that image.

HOW TO STOP HUMANS KILLING EACH OTHER WHEN IT'S PRETEND

Multiplayer online games are all the rage. In these games you sign in to a community of players who could be located anywhere in the world and a matchmaking algorithm forms you into teams. You don't know the other people in your team or the people on the other teams. They are just screen names attached to (usually military) props (like tanks, ships, soldiers etc.). Your team then does battle against the other team until one team wins and then the process is repeated and you are once again thrown into a new team of strangers.

These games go for maximum realism, so the weaponry you are virtually using is just as capable of killing your team-mates as it is of killing the enemy. This means these games have a bit of a problem with psychopathic killers. Since usually most of your team is visible to you but the enemy may not be, the easy way to get points is to simply shoot your team-mates.

Most games have some sort of system for reporting this kind of behaviour and rely on community shaming to stop it. But, as we know, shame won't stop someone who feels no remorse. Some of the latest versions of these games now include the algorithmic version of an empathy feedback loop. If you start shooting team-mates eventually you will reach a threshold (to allow for accidents) and then the damage will be deducted from your score rather than theirs. In other words, if you inflict harm, you will be harmed. Psychopathic team killers are quickly eliminated from the game because by shooting team-mates they are shooting themselves.

The cost to society

Until relatively recently the societal cost of psychopathy was minimal. Human societies prior to the industrial revolution were largely collectivist. People lived together their whole lives. They raised their families together. They were schooled together. They worshipped together. And they worked together. The research clearly shows that collectivist societies force psychopaths to conform to group norms. It's harder on the psychopaths because they have to spend their lives pretending to be normal and constantly fighting their impulses. But it's much easier on society because the destruction they bring is heavily suppressed. Collectivist societies are like a train running on a track. You can be as different as you like, but everybody is going in the same direction at the same pace.

'In an unregulated world, the least-principled people rise to the top. And there are none who are less principled than corporate psychopaths.' – Brian Basham, journalist writing on the roots of the Global Financial Crisis

The exponential growth in wealth brought about by the economics of capitalism has, however, driven every society it touches towards full individualism. There is no railway line in an individualist society, just a vast desert. And everybody is issued with a personal vehicle and told to make their way across it however they think is best. But, remember, a psychopath will have no compunction stealing your vehicle and leaving you to die if there is an advantage to them in doing so.

We've even invented fake people who are psychopaths by design so they make even more money. The modern company is a collective of individuals who are largely empaths. It is required by law to be measured by how successfully it advances its interest and delivers a financial return to its owners. It is not required to have empathy for any other person (fake or otherwise) other than as mandated by the law. As far as a company is concerned if its behaviour is not prohibited by the law, it is permitted.

And if its employees behave immorally then it has plausible deniability because it tells them to obey the law. The corporation literally has no moral compass. There is no gut instinct against causing harm that prevents it from chasing immediate reward. It allows a collective of empaths to behave more like a psychopath individually and collectively. We need look no further than the tobacco, finance, processed food, gambling and pharmaceutical industries for multiple examples of this dynamic in action. 'Greed is good.' 'Business is business.' Etc.

Communal property forces communal behaviour. As a society becomes more capitalist it becomes more individualist. The inevitable consequence is that we stop sharing stuff. We stop because we no longer need to share to have nice things. Why go to the public pool when you can have one of your own? Why take the bus when you can own (or at least lease) your own car? Why make your kids share a room or <gasp> a bathroom, when you can afford to give them one of their own?

With the loss of communal property, we lose the communal attitudes which are necessary to preserve and maintain it. When this happens on a large scale the fabric of society begins to fray. When immunisation is a community obligation, delivered to every member of a community by the community, it happens by default. You need to take positive action to opt out. But once it becomes an individual's responsibility to arrange and pay for it, less and less people participate. It becomes opt-in. Slowly but surely the herd immunity drops and we eventually all pay the cost. The same goes for education, health care, even organ donation.

Individualistic cultures (such as Australia) force people to be competitive and self-reliant. Independence and self-confidence are encouraged at every turn. Inevitably short-lived personal and business relationships are common. Communal cultures, on the other hand, require individuals to contribute to the maintenance of communal assets from which everyone will eventually benefit. Dependence and loyalty are encouraged at every turn. All group members will look out for every other member's welfare. Long-term stable relationships are the norm because we are all on the same train going to the same place at the same speed.

In individualist cultures, those requirements combine to produce anonymity, competition, self-absorption, superficiality, promiscuity, and a lack of responsibility for others. This is a perfect recipe for higher levels of crime, deception, manipulation and parasitic behaviour. In communal or collectivist societies, all of these will be repressed.

In short, in an individualistic society, we all start behaving like psychopaths and that makes the real psychopaths' job so much easier. The key to a psychopath being able to successfully exploit our emotional 'weaknesses' is for us not to know they are a psychopath until it is too late. In an individualistic society, all the sheep are in wolves' clothing. It is so much easier for a psychopath to hide in a society where everyone behaves like she does. But in a collectivist society, a psychopath sticks out like the proverbial canine scrotum (if they want to be themselves).

We trust nobody

When we are individualistic in our approach, we cannot trust anyone. We know that everyone else is out for themselves. This causes us to behave in an unco-operative way, which only increases the levels of distrust in our community.

Since 2000 the world's largest ad agency, Edelman, has been compiling what it calls the 'Trust Barometer'. The barometer is a survey taken by 33,000 respondents in twenty-eight countries. It divides respondents into 'informed public' and general respondents. The informed public are university educated people over twenty-five who earn in the top twenty-five percent of incomes in their country. They represent thirteen percent of the global population surveyed.

In the 2017 survey, fifty-four percent of the informed Australian public still trusted institutions but just forty percent of the rest of the population did. In the US those numbers were sixty-eight percent and forty-seven percent respectively.

This evaporation of trust means that we begin to believe the system is biased in favour of elites and indifferent to the people they serve. We lose hope because we no longer believe that hard work will be rewarded or that our children will have a better life. It creates in us a desire for change, any change because it couldn't be worse than what we've got.

The barometer has recorded a steady drop in our trust in government, experts, media and leadership and an acceleration of the divergence between the degree to which the informed public trust in those institutions as compared to the rest of us. Edelman asserts that, 'Current populist movements are fuelled by a lack of trust in the system.'

In Australia, just eleven percent of people surveyed believed the system was working. This is the same number as in the UK and the US, the two countries that have recently voted in favour of populist movements.

Invariably the people exploiting our distrust in mainstream systems are psychopaths who have spied an opportunity to take a shortcut to power and money. By default, capitalism drives individualism, which in turn drives the destruction of community values, co-operation and trust. When that happens empaths are cannon fodder in psychopathic power games and our entire society becomes a happy hunting ground for psychopaths.

But it need not be so. We can change the way we behave towards each other. The required change is neither difficult nor expensive, but it could significantly curtail the power of psychopaths and create a better society for us all.

CONCLUSION

Over the last 200 years, industrial economics has forced us into a state of being that does not require the machinery our brains carefully evolved over the previous ten millennia. In this highly competitive, individualistic world you are better off without morals holding you back. Mind you, it might not be a world you'd care to live in. In this world, everybody is dispensable and every gain is at the expense of somebody else's loss. It is the least that humans can be and the least that they can achieve.

But you can change it. If you decide to quit sugar, the only thing you are changing is your diet. But if enough of the people you know follow your lead and their friends follow them and so on, before long, Coca-Cola will be selling sparkling water instead of soft drink. Local action can have communal effects.

You need look no further than the examples of Hewlett-Packard, Intel and Wetherill Associates in earlier chapters to see that in action. Those organisations decided that ethics were their guiding lights rather than economic gain. This did not mean they were not interested in profit, just that it was considered *after* they had decided to do the right thing. That changed the priority. Rather than it being 'Make a profit and then do the right thing if possible', it became 'Do the right thing and make a profit if possible'.

They insisted on individual honesty, open communication and community values. They insisted on behaving to the highest ethical standards at all times, without exception. Money was no longer the measure, honesty was. They accepted no breaches of those standards. And, in each case, the rewards followed. Perhaps like the farmer who overused the commons they could have made more in the short term by not being honest, but by being honest, they preserved the commons. For them, the commons was their reputation. And by preserving that commons, they were able to farm it in perpetuity.

We can all do this. We can all behave in a way that is unimpeachable. We can all resist the temptation for short-term, but often questionable, gain. We can all choose to act in accordance with the Golden Rule, even if we know we can talk our way out of it and even if we know we can benefit if we don't. We can all choose to use the wiring we have so painstakingly evolved to make us better as a group than we ever could be as individuals.

If enough of us do that, our society will be completely psychopath proof. No, they will not be cured. But they will have no choice but to act in accordance with our rules rather than have us act in accordance with theirs. And even if you and I are the only people who do this, then we will have at least psychopath-proofed ourselves. A psychopath has no power over an honest person who is not prepared to play their manipulative games.

At its core, this book is not about psychopaths. It's about you. It's about you and the society you want to be part of. It's about the values you want that society to have. It's a DIY guide to building a genuinely psychopath-proof community and a genuinely psychopath-proof you.

Do not lie. Do not tolerate being lied to. No, I mean *really* don't tolerate it. And remember *your* word must also be *your* deed. Be savvy and a little bit cynical of those who ask for your allegiance. Judge them by their actions, not their words, and have no trust in the sudden epiphany and apology when they are caught in a lie. The leopard rarely changes its spots.

Instead, put your trust in people with proven track records of passion and honesty, rather than those who wear the coloured ribbon of today's popular cause. Look for substance and avoid those who value style more. Be careful how you define success: money is not the measure. Like assessing the quality of anything based on its price, using the appearance of money is a lazy and unreliable way to vet those you should trust. It is too easy to simulate having it and, in any case, the world is full of ill-gotten, short-lived gains.

Step away from the water-cooler that is modern social media. Discuss ideas. Discuss movies. Discuss music. But don't indulge in gossip aimed at demeaning others. And always play the ball not the man – argue about the ideas, not the person who has them.

Yes, I have gone beyond my brief, but all of these are features, and the inevitable consequence, of moving us to a fundamentally more honest society, one which gives no sustenance to a psychopathic world-view. It is a society we can achieve and it starts with just one person.

You.

GUIDE TO INFO-BOXES

CASE STUDIES

TESTS AND TIPS

Figures

NOTES

Chapter One: A Short History of Psychopathy

Page

14   In late nineteenth-century America, the term . . .: WF Evans, *Mental Medicine: A theoretical and practical treatise*, Carter & Pettee, Boston, 1873.

14   Personality disordered people account for between . . .: Bret S Steka, Christoph U Correll, 'A Guide to DSM-5', *Disclosures*, May 2013, and 'Personality Disorders', *International Encylcopedia of the Behavioural and Social Sciences*, 2001, pp. 11301–11308.

15   The disorders are . . .: Neel Burton, 'The Ten Personality Disorders', *Psychology Today*, posted 29 May 2012, www.psychologytoday.com

15   Up until the 1930s, describing someone . . .: G. E. Partridge, 'Current Conceptions of Psychopathic Personality', *The American Journal of Psychiatry*, 1930 July; 1(87), pp. 53–99

16   During the 1930s courts and law-makers . . .: Ena Chadha, '"Mentally Defectives" Not Welcome: Mental Disability In Canadian Immigration Law, 1859–1927', *Disability Studies Quarterly*, vol. 28, no. 1, 2008, Tamara Lave, 'Only Yesterday: The Rise and Fall of Twentieth Century Sexual Psychopath Laws', *Louisiana Law Review*, vol. 69, no. 3, Spring 2009, http://dsq-sds.org/article/view/67/67

16   By World War II, psychologists, despairing at the multiple . . .: http://research. omicsgroup.org/index.php/George_E._Partridge

17   The book focused on a personality type . . .: Cleckley, Hervey, *The Mask of Sanity: An Attempt to Clarify Some Issues about the So-Called Psychopathic Personality*, Emily S. Cleckley, Saint Louis, Missouri, 5th edition, 1988.

Chapter One: A Short History of Psychopathy (cont.)
Page

18   But this didn't stop Cleckley continuing . . .: ibid, pp. 249–252.

18   Hare's PCLs are now widely used . . .: Elizabeth Cauffman, Eva R. Kimonis, Julia Dmitrieva, and Kathryn C. Monahan, 'A Multimethod Assessment of Juvenile Psychopathy: Comparing the Predictive Utility of the PCL:YV, YPI, and NEO PRI', *Psychological Assessment*, vol. 21, no. 4, 2009, pp. 528–542. http://dx.doi.org/10.1037/a0017367 Walters GD, Knight RA, Grann M, Dahle KP, 'Incremental validity of the Psychopathy Checklist facet scores: predicting release outcome in six samples', *Journal of Abnormal Psychology*, May 2008, vol. 117, no. 2, pp. 396–405. doi:10.1037/0021-843X.117.2.396

18   People who score high on the PCL are . . .: Martens, Willem, 'The problem with Robert Hare's psychopathy checklist: Incorrect conclusions, high risk of misuse, and lack of reliability', *Medicine and Law*, vol. 27, no. 2, 2008, pp. 449–62.

18   The checklist is made up of twenty personality traits . . .: Hare, Robert, 'A research scale for the assessment of psychopathy in criminal populations', *Personality and Individual Differences*, vol. 1, no. 2, 1980, pp. 111–19, https://doi.org/10.1016/0191-8869(80)90028-8

19   The average person scores between 3 and 6 . . .: Len Sperry (ed.), *Mental Health and Mental Disorders: An Encyclopedia of Conditions, Treatments, and Well-Being*, Greenwood, Santa Barbara, California, 2015.

19   A total score of 30 or over in . . .: Skeem, J. L.; Polaschek, D. L. L.; Patrick, C. J.; Lilienfeld, S. O., 'Psychopathic Personality: Bridging the Gap Between Scientific Evidence and Public Policy', *Psychological Science in the Public Interest*, 2011, vol. 12, no. 3, pp. 95–162. doi:10.1177/1529100611426706. Semple, David, *The Oxford Handbook of Psychiatry*, Oxford University Press, Oxford, 2005, pp. 448–9.

21   People who score highly on Facets 1 . . .: Harpur, Timothy J., Hare, Robert D., Hakstian, A. Ralph, 'Two-factor conceptualization of psychopathy: Construct validity and assessment implications', *Psychological Assessment: A Journal of Consulting and Clinical Psychology*, vol. 1, no. 1, 1989, pp. 6–17.

21   The DSM description of ASPD is long-winded and opaque . . .: 'To diagnose antisocial personality disorder, the following criteria must be met: A. Significant impairments in personality functioning manifest by: 1. Impairments in self functioning (a or b): a. Identity: Ego-centrism; self-esteem derived from personal gain, power, or pleasure. b. Self-direction: Goal-setting based on personal gratification; absence of prosocial internal standards associated with failure to conform to lawful or culturally normative ethical behavior. AND 2. Impairments in interpersonal functioning (a or b): a. Empathy: Lack of concern for feelings, needs, or suffering of others; lack of remorse after hurting or mistreating another. b. Intimacy: Incapacity for mutually intimate relationships, as exploitation is a primary means of relating to others, including by deceit and coercion; use of dominance or intimidation to control others.' American Psychiatric Association, *Diagnostic and Statistical Manual of Mental Disorders* (5th Edition), Washington, DC, 2013.

21   . . . the Mayo Clinic has provided this handy summary . . .: Mayo Clinic, Antisocial Personality Disorder, www.mayoclinic.org

Chapter One: A Short History of Psychopathy (cont.)

Page

22 He says that eighty-five percent of criminals . . .: Hare, Robert D. *Without Conscience: The Disturbing World of Psychopaths Among Us*, Pocket Books, New York, 1993.

22 Psychopaths are generally regarded by psychologists . . .: Dingfelder, Sadie F., 'Treatment for the "untreatable"', *Monitor on Psychology*, March 2004, vol. 35, no. 3. Bonn, Scott, 'Psychopathic Criminals Cannot be Cured', *Psychology Today*, 11 August 2014, www.psychologytoday.com

24 In October 2016, Samuel Velasco Gurrola from El Paso . . .: Lashay Wesley, 'El Paso man found guilty in murder-for-hire case', 18 October 2016, www.cbs4local.com

24 That didn't work out, so he had . . .: Lashay Wesley, 'Former husband of woman killed in alleged murder-for-hire plot takes the stand', 14 October 2016, www.cbs4local.com

24 As early as 1964, researchers had . . .: McCord, William Maxwell and McCord, Joan, *The psychopath: An essay on the criminal mind*, Van Nostrand, Princeton, 1964.

25 In 1901 Ivan Pavlov showed that a dog's . . .: https://www.nobelprize.org/educational/medicine/pavlov/readmore.html

25 In 1920, psychologist Dr John Watson . . .: Watson, John B and Rayner, Rosalie, 'Conditioned Emotional Reactions', *Journal of Experimental Psychology*, vol. 3, no. 1, pp. 1–14. You can watch the film of the experiment here: https://www.youtube.com/watch?v=9hBfnXACsOI

26 The hunt took the better part of a century . . .: Powell, Russell A.; Digdon, Nancy; Harris, Ben; Smithson, Christopher, 'Correcting the record on Watson, Rayner, and Little Albert: Albert Barger as "Psychology's lost boy"', *American Psychologist*, vol. 69, no. 6, 2014, pp. 600–611. http://dx.doi.org/10.1037/a0036854

27 In the late 1970s and early 1980s fear conditioning . . .: Rothemund, Y et al, 'Fear conditioning in psychopaths: Event-related potentials and peripheral measures', *Biological Psychology*, vol. 90, no. 1, 2012, pp. 50–59 http://doi.org/10.1016/j.biopsycho.2012.02.011

27 All the subjects knew what was coming . . .: Hare, R. D., 'Psychopathy and Physiological Activity During Anticipation of an Aversive Stimulus in a Distraction Paradigm', *Psychophysiology*, vol. 19, 1982, pp. 266–271. doi:10.1111/j.1469-8986.1982.tb02559.x

28 Further studies in the 1990s experimented with . . .: A Scerbo et al, 'Reward Dominance and Passive Avoidance Learning in Adolescent Psychopaths', *Journal of Abnormal Child Psychology*, vol. 18, no. 4, 1990, pp. 451–463. Dikman, Z and Allen, J, 'Error Monitoring during reward and avoidance learning in high- and low-socialized individuals', *Psychophysiology*, vol. 37, no. 1, 2000, pp. 43–54.

28 Multiple studies on very divergent populations have . . .: Epstein MK, Poythress NG, Brandon KO, 'The Self-Report Psychopathy Scale and passive avoidance learning: a validation study of race and gender effects', *Assessment*, vol. 13, no. 2, pp. 197–207. doi:10.1177/1073191105284992

29 Psychopaths and empaths both fail to pick . . .: Newman, J and Kosson, D, 'Passive Avoidance Learning in Psychopathic and Nonpsychopathic Offenders', *Journal of Abnormal Psychology*, 1986, vol. 95, no. 3, pp. 252–56.

Chapter One: A Short History of Psychopathy (cont.)

Page

29   Depressives exaggerate the negative and minimize the positive. . .: Beck, A.T.,
      Steer, R.A., & Brown, G.K, *Manual for the Beck Depression Inventory-II*,
      Psychological Corporation, San Antonio, 1996.

29   A psychopath is characterised by excessive social approach . . .: Arnett, P, Smith, S
      and Newman, J, 'Approach and Avoidance Motivation in Psychopathic Criminal
      Offenders During Passive Avoidance', *Journal of Personality and Social Psychology*,
      1997, vol. 72, no. 6, pp. 1413–1428.

29   This is what the psychologists call . . .: Avila, César, 'Distinguishing BIS-mediated
      and BAS-mediated disinhibition mechanisms: A comparison of disinhibition
      models of Gray (1981, 1987) and of Patterson and Newman (1993)', *Journal of
      Personality and Social Psychology*, vol. 80, no. 2, 2001, pp. 311–324. http://dx.doi.
      org/10.1037/0022-3514.80.2.311

29   In a psychopath, the activation system is dominant and pushes them toward
      impulsive action . . .: Arnett, P, Smith, S and Newman, J, 'Approach and Avoidance
      Motivation in Psychopathic Criminal Offenders During Passive Avoidance', *Journal
      of Personality and Social Psychology*, 1997, vol. 72, no. 6, pp. 1413–1428.

29   A psychopath is as capable of becoming depressed . . .: Lovelace, L and Gannon, L,
      'Psychopathy and depression: mutually exclusive constructs?', *Journal of Behavior
      Therapy and Experimental Psychiatry*, vol. 30, no. 3, September 1999, Pages 169–176.

30   The studies also show that when psychopaths are presented . . .: Arnett, P,
      'Autonomic Responsivity In Psychopaths: A Critical Review And Theoretical
      Proposal', *Clinical Psychology Review*, vol. 17, no. 8, 1997, pp. 903–936.

31   Wisconsin card sort test . . .: Screenshot of PEBL (Psychology Experiment Building
      Language) software running Wisconsin Card Sort.

31   This type of study shows subjects cards . . .: Newman, J.P., 'Reaction to punishment
      in extraverts and psychopaths: Implications for the impulsive behavior of disinhibited
      individuals', *Journal of Research in Personality*, vol. 21, no. 4, December 1987,
      pp. 464–480, http://www.sciencedirect.com/science/article/pii/009265668790033X

32   Psychopaths universally do much worse on this sort of study than empaths . . .:
      Yang, Yaling et al, 'Abnormal Structural Correlates of Response Perseveration
      in Individuals With Psychopathy', *The Journal of Neuropsychiatry and Clinical
      Neurosciences*, vol. 23, no. 1, 2011, pp. 107–110.

32   If the subjects are just told a card placement . . .: ibid.

35   One popular psychological description says . . . Plutchik, Robert, 'The circumplex as
      a general model of the structure of emotions and personality', in Circumplex Models
      of personality and emotions, Plutchik, R (Ed); Conte, Hope R. (Ed), Washington, DC,
      US: American Psychological Association, doi:10.1037/10261-001

38   At the time of her death, in 1997 . . .: Serge Larivée, Carole Sénéchal, Geneviève
      Chénard, 'Les côtés ténébreux de Mère Teresa', *Studies in Religion/sciences
      religieuses*, January 15 2013, issue 42. Dicker, Ron, 'Mother Teresa Humanitarian
      Image A "Myth", New Study Says', *The Huffington Post*, 5 March 2013.

38   The missions were described as 'human warehouses'. . .: Aroup Chatterjee, *Mother
      Teresa, The Final Verdict*, Meteor Books, Michigan, 2003, pp. 196–197. You can
      see them in Christopher Hitchens' expose on Mother Teresa: https://www.youtube.
      com/watch?v=65JxnUW7Wk4

Chapter One: A Short History of Psychopathy (cont.)

Page

38   This was in spite of the fact that Mother . . .: Wuellenweber, Walter, 'Mother Teresa: Where are her millions?' reprinted from *Stern* magazine, 1998, http://www.srai.org/mother-teresa-where-are-her-millions/

39   She explained why that care was not . . .: 'Mother Teresa anything but a saint . . .' *Udemnouvelles*, 3 January 2013, http://nouvelles.umontreal.ca/en/article/2013/03/01/mother-teresa-anything-but-a-saint/ Hitchens, Christopher, *The Missionary Position: Mother Teresa in theory and in practice*, Verso, London/New York, 1995, p.11.

39   When asked how the poor could. . .: ibid, p.95.

39   However she lived a lavish lifestyle . . .: Chatterjee, pp. 2–14.

39   Teresa frequently lied about her achievements . . .: Krishna Dutta, 'Saint of the gutters with friends in high places', *Times Higher Education World University Rankings,* May 16, 2003, https://www.timeshighereducation.com/books/saint-of-the-gutters-with-friends-in-high-places/176802.article

39   The reality was very different . . .: Chatterjee, pp. 179–180.

39   She claimed to have 102 family assistance centres . . .: ibid.

40   Ancient historians describe Caligula as being . . .: Suetonius, *Lives of the Twelve Caesars*, Loeb Classical Library, 1913, http://penelope.uchicago.edu/Thayer/e/roman/texts/suetonius/12caesars/caligula*.html

40   It's hard to diagnose someone two millennia . . .: Eric Pace, 'IDEAS & TRENDS; Scholarship Yields A New Caligula, Who Is Merely Obnoxious', *New York Times*, April 1, 1990, http://www.nytimes.com/1990/04/01/weekinreview/ideas-trends-scholarship-yields-a-new-caligula-who-is-merely-obnoxious.html

41   Former Obama aide David Plouffe told CNN . . .: Elisha Fieldstadt, 'Ex-Obama Campaign Manager David Plouffe Calls Donald Trump a "Psychopath"', NBC News, 28 August 2016.

41   Tony Schwartz, the co-author of Trump's autobiography . . .: Mayer, Jane, 'Donald Trump's Ghostwriter Tells All', *New Yorker*, 25 July 2016.

41   In 2012, a US Anti-Doping Agency investigation . . .: Statement From USADA CEO Travis T. Tygart Regarding The U.S. Postal Service Pro Cycling Team Doping Conspiracy, 10 October 2012, http://cyclinginvestigation.usada.org/

42   During the interview, Oprah put to Lance . . .: Lance Armstrong and Oprah Winfrey interview transcript, BBC Sport, 18 January 2013, http://www.bbc.com/sport/cycling/21065539

42   For her trouble she faced constant vilification . . .: You can read Betsy Andreu's full affidavit here: http://d3epuodzu3wuis.cloudfront.net/Andreu+Betsy+Affidavit.pdf

42   In 2015 Betsy described Lance . . .: Daniel McMahon, 'The woman who helped bring down Lance Armstrong wishes he'd "shut his mouth and go away forever" as he returns to the Tour de France', *Business Insider,* 16 July 2015 https://www.businessinsider.com.au/betsy-andreu-interview-lance-armstrong-tour-de-france-2015-7?r=US&IR=T

42   Psychologist and popular writer on psychopathy . . .: Dutton, Kevin, 'Would you vote for a Psychopath?' *Scientific American Mind*, September 2016.

42   Dutton used an abbreviated version of the PPI- R test . . .: The PPI is based on the work by Cleckley and Hare and asks respondents to answer a series of statements about themselves on a 4 point scale ('False', 'Mostly False', 'Mostly True', 'True') – the statements align with 8 categories (or Factors) – Lack of Empathy, Charm, Impulsivity, Fearlessness, Blaming others, social nonconformity and stress immunity.

Chapter One: A Short History of Psychopathy (cont.)

Page

43   Some researchers on the evolution of trust famously . . .: Wilson DS, Wilson EO, 'Rethinking the theoretical foundation of sociobiology.' *Quarterly Review of Biology*, vol. 82, no. 4, 2007, pp. 327–48.

44   A recent study of film depictions of psychopaths . . .: Leistedt, S and Linkowski, P, 'Psychopathy and the Cinema: Fact or Fiction?' *Journal of Forensic Sciences*, 13 December 2013, doi:10.1111/1556-4029.12359

44   Perhaps rather disturbingly, the director . . .: Vieira, Anthony, 'Wall Street review', 23 September 2010, https://thefilmstage.com/reviews/review-wall-street-money-never-sleeps/

Chapter Two: Empathy: The Missing Element

Page

45   *Einfühlung* was first used by Robert Vischer . . .: Vischer, Robert, *Empathy, Form, and Space: Problems in German Aesthetics, 1873–1893*, Getty Center for the History of Art and Humanities, 1994.

45   But Edward Titchener, a British psychologist . . .: Titchener EB, *Lectures on the experimental psychology of the thought- processes*, The MacMillan Company, New York, 1909.

45   The current dictionary definition is . . .: http://www.merriam-webster.com/dictionary/empathy

46   It takes us a full two years to display the . . .: Hoffman, M.L., *Empathy and Moral Development*, Cambridge University Press, Cambridge, 2000.

46   And one year olds have a good enough . . .: Onishi, Kristine H., and Renée Baillargeon. 'Do 15-Month-Old Infants Understand False Beliefs?' *Science (New York, N.y.)* 308.5719 (2005): 255–258. Decety, J and Meyer, M 'From emotion resonance to empathic understanding: A social developmental neuroscience account', *Development and Psychopathology*, vol. 20, no. 4, October 2008, pp. 1053–1080.

46   Non-human animals don't run Theory of Mind simulations . . .: van der Vaart, E and Hemelrijk, C, '"Theory of mind" in animals: ways to make progress', Synthese, vol. 191, no. 3, February 2014, doi:10.1007/s11229-012-0170-3

47   Asperger's description of the autistic psychopath was . . .: Asperger, H. 'Die "Autistischen Psychopathen" im Kindesalter', Archiv f. Psychiatrie (1944) 117: 76. doi:10.1007/BF01837709

49   Even though the creators of the show deny . . .: 'The Big Bang Controversy: Is Sheldon Autistic?' *Autism Daily Newcast*, 4 July 2013, http://www.autismdailynewcast.com

49   People with those symptoms are now diagnosed . . .: 'DSM-V What Changes May Mean', Autism.com, https://www.autism.com

49   People with Asperger's lack cognitive empathy . . .: 'Differentiating Cognitive and Emotional Empathy in Individuals with Asperger Syndrome', Max Planck Institute for Human Development.

50   People who like to study such things . . .: Blair, R, 'Empathic dysfunction in psychopathic individuals', in F. D. Farrow & R. Woodruff (eds.), *Empathy in mental illness*. Cambridge University Press, 2007, pp. 3–16. Blair et al, 'Theory of Mind in the psychopath', *Journal of Forensic Psychiatry*, vol. 7, no. 1, 1996, pp. 15–25, doi:10.1080/09585189608409914

Chapter Two: Empathy: The Missing Element (cont.)

Page

50   Recent advances in brain imaging technology . . .: Shamay-Tsoory SG, 'The neural bases for empathy', *Neuroscientist*, vol. 17, no. 1, 2011 pp. 18–24. doi:10.1177/1073858410379268.

51   But a psychopath has no sense of this. . . .: R.J.R. Blair, 'Responding to the emotions of others: Dissociating forms of empathy through the study of typical and psychiatric populations', *Consciousness and Cognition*, vol. 14, 2005, pp. 698–718

51   That gap in timing is almost imperceptible but many empaths . . .: Williamson, S., Harpur, T. J. and Hare, R. D., 'Abnormal Processing of Affective Words by Psychopaths', *Psychophysiology*, vol. 28, 1991, pp. 260–273. doi:10.1111/j.1469-8986. 1991.tb02192.x

51   A recent study scanned brain function . . .: Nummenmaa L, Hirvonen J, Parkkola R, Hietanen JK, 'Is emotional contagion special? An fMRI study on neural systems for affective and cognitive empathy,' *Neuroimage*, vol. 43, no. 3, 2008, pp. 571–80. doi:10.1016/j.neuroimage.2008.08.014.

52   Scientists have known since the 1940s . . .: Price Heusner, A, 'Yawning And Associated Phenomena', *Physiological Reviews*, vol. 26, no. 1, 1946, pp. 156–168.

52   We are five times as likely to yawn . . .: Norscia I, Palagi E, 'Yawn Contagion and Empathy in *Homo sapiens*', PLoS ONE, vol. 6, no. 12, 2011, e28472. doi:10.1371/ journal.pone.0028472

53   They seem to be able to screen out . . .: Sadeh, Naomi, and Edelyn Verona, 'Psychopathic Personality Traits Associated with Abnormal Selective Attention and Impaired Cognitive Control', *Neuropsychology*, vol. 22, no. 5, 2008, pp. 669–680.

53   In one study, when psychopaths . . .: Jutai, J. W. and Hare, R. D, 'Psychopathy and Selective Attention During Performance of a Comp Perceptual-Motor Task,' *Psychophysiology*, vol. 20, 1983, pp. 146–151. doi:10.1111/j.1469-8986.1983. tb03280.x

54   Hours after the planes hit . . .: You can watch the interview here: https://www. youtube.com/watch?v=PcKlPhFIE7w

54   In answer to Marcus's concern about . . .: Kruse, Michael, 'What Trump and Clinton Did on 9/11', *Politico* magazine, 10 September 2016.

55   Until very recently the study of . . .: Kiehl, Kent A., and Morris B. Hoffman, 'The Criminal Psychopath: History, Neuroscience, Treatment, And Economics,' *Jurimetrics*, 51, 2011, pp. 355–397.

56   The majority view is there is no cure but that . . .: Bonn, Scott, 'Psychopathic Criminals Cannot Be Cured', *Psychology Today*, 11 August 2014, www. psychologytoday.com

56   And, even where we know it to be true, the . . .: Craparo, Giuseppe, Adriano Schimmenti, and Vincenzo Caretti, 'Traumatic Experiences in Childhood and Psychopathy: A Study on a Sample of Violent Offenders from Italy', *European Journal of Psychotraumatology*, 4, 2013, doi:10.3402/ejpt.v4i0.21471

56   Human brains quadruple in size between ..: Dekaban, A. S. and Sadowsky, D, 'Changes in brain weights during the span of human life: Relation of brain weights to body heights and body weights', *Annals of Neurology*, 4 1978, pp. 345–356. doi:10.1002/ana.410040410

56   Pathways are constantly being built and . . .: Stiles, Joan, and Terry L. Jernigan, 'The Basics of Brain Development', *Neuropsychology Review*, vol. 20, no. 4, 2010, pp. 327–348.

57   Research has clearly shown that the pathways . . .: Kolb, Bryan, and Robbin Gibb, 'Brain Plasticity and Behaviour in the Developing Brain,' Ed. Margaret Clarke and Laura Ghali, *Journal of the Canadian Academy of Child and Adolescent Psychiatry*, vol. 20, no. 4, 2011, pp. 265–276.

58   He told one biographer he performed his . . .: Nelson, Polly, *Defending the Devil: My Story As Ted Bundy's Last Lawyer*, William Morrow and Co, New York, 1994.

58   He told a psychologist he killed . . .: Sullivan, Kevin M., *The Bundy Murders: a comprehensive history*, McFarland & Co, North Carolina, 2009, p.57. Keppel, Robert, *The Riverman: Ted Bundy and I Hunt for the Green River Killer*, Pocket Books, New York, 2010.

58   Some investigators think he actually . . .: ibid.

58   Bipolar Disorder (manic depression that causes . . .: Samuel, Douglas B. and Widiger, Thomas A., 'Describing Ted Bundy's Personality and Working towards DSM-V', *Independent Practitioner*, 2007, vol. 27, no. 1, pp. 20–22.

59   He frequently told FBI interviewers and doctors . . .: Aynesworth, Hugh, *Ted Bundy: Conversations with a Killer*, Authorlink, New York, 2000.

59   One of his examining psychiatrists admitted . . .: Von Drehle, David, *Among the Lowest of the Dead: The Culture on Death Row* Crown, New York, New Jersey, 1995.

59   In the interview, Bundy blamed . . .: You can watch the interview on Vimeo here: https://vimeo.com/49018764

59   In the early 1970s psychologists led by . . .: Ekman P, Friesen WV., 'Constants across cultures in the face and emotion', *Journal of Personality and Social Psychology*, vol. 17, no. 2, 1971, pp. 124–9.

59   In his book *The Expression of Emotions* . . .: Darwin, Charles, *The Expression of the Emotions in Man and Animals*, D. Appleton & Company, New York, 1872.

60   In 1939, Dr Heinrich Kluver, a . . .: National Academy of Science, *Biographical Memoirs vol. 73*, National Academy Press, Washington DC, 1998, pp. 288–305.

60   Native Americans have been 'tripping' . . .: El-Seedi, Hesham et al, 'Prehistoric peyote use: Alkaloid analysis and radiocarbon dating of archaeological specimens of Lophophora from Texas', *Journal of Ethnopharmacology*, vol. 101, 1–3, 2005, pp. 238–42, doi:10.1016/j.jep.2005.04.022

61   They all still had normal vision . . .: Bourtchouladze, Rusiko, *Memories Are Made of This: How Memory Works in Humans and Animals*, Columbia University Press, 2003.

61   This he described as an inability . . .: Klüver, H.; Bucy, P. C. , '"Psychic blindness" and other symptoms following bilateral temporal lobectomy in Rhesus monkeys', *American Journal of Physiology*, vol. 119, 1937, pp. 352–353.

61   They attempted to eat inappropriate . . .: Atlay, Kemal, 'The real reason why Labradors eat so much', *The New Daily*, 8 May 2016.

61   Kluver–Bucy syndrome (as it was . . .: Terzian H, Ore GD, 'Syndrome of Klüver and Bucy; reproduced in man by bilateral removal of the temporal lobes', *Neurology*, vol. 5, no. 6, 1955, pp. 373–80.

Chapter Two: Empathy: The Missing Element (cont.)
Page

61 The primary symptoms in humans . . .: Tsapkini, Kyrana, Constantine E. Frangakis, and Argye E. Hillis, 'The Function of the Left Anterior Temporal Pole: Evidence from Acute Stroke and Infarct Volume', Brain, vol. 134, no. 10, 2011, pp. 3094–3105.

61 By 1967 more monkey experiments . . .: Arthur Kling & Phillip C. Green, 'Effects of Neonatal Amygdalectomy in the Maternally Reared and Maternally Deprived Macaque', Nature, 213, 1967, pp. 742–743 doi:10.1038/213742b0

62 Research in animals and humans has . . .: Gallagher M, Chiba AA, 'The amygdala and emotion', Current Opinion in Neurobiology, vol. 6, no. 2, 1996, pp. 221–7.

62 A strong thread in psychology literature . . .: Rutter, M. 'Commentary: What is the meaning and utility of the psychopathy concept?' Journal of Abnormal Child Psychology, 33, pp. 499–503. McCrory E, De Brito SA, Viding E, 'The link between child abuse and psychopathology: a review of neurobiological and genetic research', Journal of the Royal Society of Medicine, vol. 105, no. 4, 2012, pp. 151–6. doi:10.1258/jrsm.2011.110222

62 But animal studies have shown that neglect . . .: Tottenham, Nim, and Margaret A. Sheridan, 'A Review of Adversity, The Amygdala and the Hippocampus: A Consideration of Developmental Timing', Frontiers in Human Neuroscience 3, 2009, 68.

62 And we know that in humans, early abuse . . .: Maheu, Françoise S. et al, 'A Preliminary Study of Medial Temporal Lobe Function in Youths with a History of Caregiver Deprivation and Emotional Neglect,' Cognitive, Affective & Behavioral Neuroscience, vol. 10, no. 1, 2010, pp. 34–49.

63 Psychologists now think that it is . . .: Markowitsch HJ. 'Differential contribution of right and left amygdala to affective information processing,' Behavioural Neurology, vol. 11, no. 4, 1998, pp. 233–244

63 Just like other parts of the human brain . . .: Uematsu A, Matsui M, Tanaka C, Takahashi T, Noguchi K, Suzuki M, Nishijo H., 'Developmental trajectories of amygdala and hippocampus from infancy to early adulthood in healthy individuals', PLoS One, vol. 7, no. 10, 2012, e46970. doi:10.1371/journal.pone.004697

63 A genuine display of fear in . . .: Marsh, Abigail A., Megan N. Kozak, and Nalini Ambady, 'Accurate Identification of Fear Facial Expressions Predicts Prosocial Behavior', Emotion (Washington, D.C.), vol. 7, no. 2, 2007, pp. 239–251.

65 In a 2008 study Georgetown University . . .: Marsh AA et al, 'Reduced amygdala response to fearful expressions in children and adolescents with callous-unemotional traits and disruptive behavior disorders', American Journal of Psychiatry, vol. 165, no. 6, 2008, pp. 712–20. doi:10.1176/appi.ajp.2007.07071145

66 That study compared MRIs of twenty-seven . . .: Yang, Yaling et al, 'Localization of Deformations Within the Amygdala in Individuals With Psychopathy,' Archives of General Psychiatry, vol. 66, no. 9, 2009, pp. 986–994.

66 In 2012 a similar study performed . . .: Gregory S, ffytche D, Simmons A, Kumari V, Howard M, Hodgins S, Blackwood N, 'The Antisocial Brain: Psychopathy Matters A Structural MRI Investigation of Antisocial Male Violent Offenders', Archives of General Psychiatry, vol. 69, no. 9, 2012, pp. 962–972. doi:10.1001/archgenpsychiatry.2012.222

Chapter Two: Empathy: The Missing Element (cont.)
Page

67   The aPFC is the most recently evolved . . .: Semendeferi K, Armstrong E, Schleicher A, Zilles K, Van Hoesen GW, 'Prefrontal cortex in humans and apes: a comparative study of area 10', *American Journal of Physical Anthropology*, vol. 114, no. 3, 2001, pp. 224–41.

67   We're still not entirely sure what . . .: Koechlin, Etienne et al, 'The role of the anterior prefrontal cortex in human cognition', *Nature* 399, May 1999, pp. 148–151, doi:10.1038/20178

68   Frontotemporal dementia (FTD) is second only . . .: Julie S. Snowden, David Neary, David M. A. Mann, 'Frontotemporal dementia', *The British Journal of Psychiatry*, vol. 180, no. 2, 2002, pp. 140–143; doi:10.1192/bjp.180.2.140

68   Recently, a more primitive form . . .: Max-Planck-Gesellschaft, 'Rare neurons linked to empathy and self-awareness discovered in monkey brains', *ScienceDaily*, 21 May 2012. <www.sciencedaily.com/releases/2012/05/120521115353.htm>

68   Scientists speculate that the spindle . . .: Dunbar, R. I. M. (1998), 'The social brain hypothesis', *Evolutionary Anthropology*, 6, pp. 178–190. doi:10.1002/(SICI) 1520-6505(1998)6:5<178::AID-EVAN5>3.0.CO;2-8. Butti C, Sherwood CC, Hakeem AY, Allman JM, Hof PR, 'Total number and volume of Von Economo neurons in the cerebral cortex of cetaceans.' *The Journal of Comparative Neurology*, 515 (2), 2009.

68   They are tightly bound up with . . .: Allman JM, Hakeem A, Erwin JM, Nimchinsky E, Hof P, 'The anterior cingulate cortex. The evolution of an interface between emotion and cognition', *Annals of the New York Academy of Sciences*, 935, 2001, pp. 107–17.

68   Recent work on the precise function . . .: Allman J, Hakeem A, Watson K. 'Two phylogenetic specializations in the human brain', *Neuroscientist*, vol. 8, no. 4, 2002, pp. 335–46.

69   Some of the more advanced parts . . .: Cauda, Franco, Giuliano Carlo Geminiani, and Alessandro Vercelli, 'Evolutionary Appearance of von Economo's Neurons in the Mammalian Cerebral Cortex', *Frontiers in Human Neuroscience*, 8, 2014, 104.

70   Spindle neurons are developed relatively late . . .: Allman JM et al,. 'The von Economo neurons in frontoinsular and anterior cingulate cortex in great apes and humans', *Brain Structure & Function*, 214(5–6), 2010, pp. 495–517. doi:10.1007/s00429-010-0254-0

70   Humans are still just as good as . . .: Shepherd, Gordon M, 'The Human Sense of Smell: Are We Better Than We Think?' *PLoS Biology*, vol. 2, no. 5, 2004, e146.

70   It is likely that the reason our . . .: Cauda F, Geminiani GC and Vercelli A (2014) 'Evolutionary appearance of von Economo's neurons in the mammalian cerebral cortex', *Frontiers in Human Neuroscience*, 8:104, 2014. doi:10.3389/fnhum.2014.00104

70   The fact that spindle neurons also . . .: Pera-Guardiola, Vanessa et al, 'Brain Structural Correlates of Emotion Recognition in Psychopaths,' Ed. Cosimo Urgesi, *PLoS ONE*, vol. 11, no. 5, 2016, e0149807

70   A 2012 review of all the . . .: Dawel A, O'Kearney R, McKone E, Palermo R, 'Not just fear and sadness: meta-analytic evidence of pervasive emotion recognition deficits for facial and vocal expressions in psychopathy,' *Neuroscience and Biobehavioural Reviews*, 36(10), 2012, pp. 2288–304. doi:10.1016/j.neubiorev.2012.08.006

Chapter Two: Empathy: The Missing Element (cont.)
Page
71   This makes sense once we know that psychopaths . . .: Ly, Martina et al, 'Cortical Thinning in Psychopathy,' *The American Journal of Psychiatry*, 169.7, 2012, doi:10.1176/appi.ajp.2012.11111627

71   Conversely, one recent study showed . . .: Brüne, Martin et al. 'Neuroanatomical Correlates of Suicide in Psychosis: The Possible Role of von Economo Neurons,' Ed. Joao B. Calixto, *PLoS ONE*, 6.6, 2011, e20936

72   Psychiatrists are quick to stress . . .: Alzforum, 'Criminal Minds: Explaining Lack of Empathy in Prison Psychopaths', 8 May 2013, www.alzforum.org

72   Criminal FTD patients are generally . . .: Mendez, Mario F, 'The Unique Predisposition to Criminal Violations in Frontotemporal Dementia', *The Journal of the American Academy of Psychiatry and the Law*, 38.3, 2010, pp. 318–323.

73   This is a description of a patient . . .: Mendez, M et al, 'Pedophilia and Temporal Lobe Disturbances', *The Journal of Neuropsychiatry and Clinical Neurosciences*, vol. 12, no. 1, 2000, pp. 71–76. Mendez, Mario F., 'The Unique Predisposition to Criminal Violations in Frontotemporal Dementia', *The Journal of the American Academy of Psychiatry and the Law*, 38.3, 2010, pp. 318–323.

74   The best we can say is that studies . . .: Kim, Eun-Joo et al, 'Selective Frontoinsular von Economo Neuron and Fork Cell Loss in Early Behavioral Variant Frontotemporal Dementia', *Cerebral Cortex (New York, NY)*, vol. 22, no. 2, 2012, pp. 251–259.

75   Societies exposed to milk as a . . .: 'Got lactase?' Understanding Evolution, http://evolution.berkeley.edu/evolibrary/news/070401_lactose

75   Societies that were not exposed . . .: US National Library of Medicine, 'Lactose Intolerance', https://ghr.nlm.nih.gov

76   In 2011 researchers in Germany . . .: Brüne, Martin et al, 'Neuroanatomical Correlates of Suicide in Psychosis: The Possible Role of von Economo Neurons,' Ed. Joao B. Calixto. *PLoS ONE*, vol. 6, no. 6, 2011, e20936

76   Perhaps it's a genetic propensity combined . . .: Blonigen, Daniel M. et al, 'Psychopathic Personality Traits: Heritability and Genetic Overlap with Internalizing and Externalizing Psychopathology,' *Psychological Medicine*, vol. 35, no. 5, 2005, pp. 637–648.

77   The direct cost of male criminal . . .: Kiehl, Kent A., and Morris B. Hoffman, 'The Criminal Psychopath: History, Neuroscience, Treatment, And Economics,' *Jurimetrics* 51, 2011, pp. 355–397.

77   The researchers assessed changes . . .: Dunlop, Boadie W. et al, 'The Effects of Sertraline on Psychopathic Traits', *International Clinical Psychopharmacology*, vol. 26, no. 6, 2011, pp. 329–337.

Chapter Three: Recognising the Everyday Psychopath
Page
81   Below is an excerpt from an interview. . .: *I, Psychopath*, DVD, director Ian Walker, 2009.

84   . . .psychopaths are extraordinarily good mimics . . .: Angel Book, et al., *Evolutionary Psychological Science*, vol. 1, no. 91, 2015, doi:10.1007/s40806-015-0012-x

Chapter Three: Recognising the Everyday Psychopath (cont.)
Page

84 Most researchers agree that between a sixth . . .: Hare Psychopathy Checklist–
    Revised (PCL–R: 2nd Edition), http://www.mhs.com/product.aspx?gr=saf&
    id=overview&prod=pcl-r2

84 Recent estimates suggest it's around . . .: Craig S. Neumann & Robert D.
    Hare, 'Psychopathic traits in a large community sample: Links to violence,
    alcohol use, and intelligence', 2008, Hare, http://www.hare.org/references/
    NeumannandHareJCCP2008.pdf

85 'I sat down and took out my clipboard' . . .: Robert Hare, 'This charming
    psychopath: How to spot social predators before they attack', *Psychology
    Today*, 1 January 1994, www.psychologytoday.com/articles/199401/charming-
    psychopath

87 Psychopaths live in the moment . . .: Kevin Dutton, 'Wisdom from psychopaths?',
    Scientific American, 1 January 2013, https://www.scientificamerican.com/article/
    wisdom-from-psychopaths/

88 'His campaign is all about him . . .: Stephen Collinson, 'Donald Trump's obsession
    with himself', CNN politics, 2 June 2016, http://edition.cnn.com/2016/06/02/
    politics/donald-trump-2016-election/index.html

90 'NAS (a Caucasian, 85-year-old . . .: Steve Balsis PhD, Nicholas R. Eaton MA, Luke
    D. Cooper MA, and Thomas F. Oltmanns PhD, 'The Presentation of Narcissistic
    Personality Disorder in an Octogenarian: Converging Evidence from Multiple
    Sources', *Clinical Gerontologist*, Vol. 34 , no. 1, 2010, doi:10.1080/07317115.2011
    .524821

90 Two days after Labor lost the 2013 election . . .: Pamela Williams, 'How Kevin
    Rudd's campaign unravelled', *Australian Financial Review,* Sep 9, 2013.

90 When Rudd had been dispatched in 2010 . . .: Paul Kelly, 'The tragedy of Kevin
    Rudd can be traced to a personality flaw', *The Australian*, Aug 23, 2014.

90 . . .and there was no shortage of people . . .: Andrew Carswell, 'Kevin Rudd–hero or
    psychopath?, *The Daily Telegraph*, 10 August 2013, http://www.dailytelegraph.com.
    au/news/nsw/kevin-rudd-hero-or-psychopath/news-story/49e8551dd478f1eb28f5a3
    3653b3ca62; and 'Kevin Rudd a "psychopathic narcissist", says Labor ally Kristina
    Keneally', The New Daily and AAP, 19 July 2016, http://thenewdaily.com.au/news/
    national/2016/07/19/rudd-psychopathic-narcissist-keneally/

90 According to the latest version of the DSM . . .: DSM-IV and DSM-5 Criteria for the
    Personality Disorders, http://www.psi.uba.ar/academica/carrerasdegrado/psicologia/
    sitios_catedras/practicas_profesionales/820_clinica_tr_personalidad_psicosis/
    material/dsm.pdf

91 The document suggested that Rudd's paranoia . . .: Michael Gordon, Tony Wright
    and Jacqueline Maley, 'Flimflam man v Dr No', Sydney Morning Herald, Aug 10,
    2013.

93 While Rudd dashed about from photo opportunity . . .: Simon Cullen, 'Kevin Rudd
    to announce plans to move naval facilities to Qld, angering NSW Premier, ABC
    News, 27 August 2013, http://www.abc.net.au/news/2013–08–27/kevin-rudd-to-
    discuss-future-naval-bases-in-northern-australia/4913870

93 'The very powerful and the very stupid . . .: Dr Who, *The Face of Evil*, part 4
    (1977).

Chapter Three: Recognising the Everyday Psychopath (cont.)
Page

93   But they are still human . . .: Christopher Patrick & William G. Iacono, 'Psychopathy, threat, and the polygraph test accuracy', abstract, *Journal of Applied Psychology*, vol. 74, no. 2, April 1989, pp. 347–355, https://experts.umn.edu/en/publications/psychopathy-threat-and-polygraph-test-accuracy

95   The paper closely tracked Trump's public statements . . .: Maggie Haberman & Alexander Burns, 'A week of whoppers from Donald Trump, *The New York Times*, 24 September 2016, https://www.nytimes.com/interactive/2016/09/24/us/elections/donald-trump-statements.html

95   The Pulitzer Prize winning political journalists . . .: Kyle Cheney et al., 'Donald Trump's week of misrepresentations, exaggerations and half-truths', *PoliticoMagazine*, 25 September 2016, http://www.politico.com/magazine/story/2016/09/2016-donald-trump-fact-check-week-214287

96   Robert Hare once asked a criminal psychopath . . .: Robert Hare, 'This Charming Psychopath', *Psychology Today*, last reviewed on June 9, 2016, https://www.psychologytoday.com/articles/199401/charming-psychopath

96   In experiments designed to test our abilities . . .: Bella DePaulo, 'Why are we so bad at detecting lies?', Psychology Today, 27 May 2013, https://www.psychologytoday.com

96   Even the people who are paid to detect lies . . .: Aldert Vrij, *Detecting lies and deceit: Pitfalls and opportunities*, 2nd edition, John Wiley & Sons, Chichester, UK, 2008.

99   In 2017 a team of researchers . . .: Gary King et al., 'How the Chinese government fabricates social media posts for strategic distraction, not engaged argument', abstract, 9 April 2017, http://gking.harvard.edu

101 'Look, when you hurt somebody . . .: Daniel McMahon, 'The woman who helped bring down Lance Armstrong wishes he'd 'shut his mouth and go away forever' as he returns to the Tour de France', *Business Insider Australia*, Jul 16, 2015, https://www.businessinsider.com.au/betsy-andreu-interview-lance-armstrong-tour-de-france-2015-7

101 Although she had clearly upset them, NAS said . . .: Steve Balsis PhD, Nicholas R. Eaton MA, Luke D. Cooper MA, and Thomas F. Oltmanns PhD, 'The Presentation of Narcissistic Personality Disorder in an Octogenarian: Converging Evidence from Multiple Sources', *Clinical Gerontologist*, Vol. 34 , no. 1, 2010, doi:10.1080/07317115.2011.524821

102 The research tells us that the average criminal psychopath . . .: M.E. Rice & G.T. Harris, 'Violent recidivism: assessing predictive validity', *Journal of Consulting and Criminal Psychology*, vol. 63, no. 3, October 1995, pp. 737–748, https://www.ncbi.nlm.nih.gov/pubmed

102 'Peter is still around, but I know I couldn't get along with him . . .: Steve Balsis PhD, Nicholas R. Eaton MA, Luke D. Cooper MA, and Thomas F. Oltmanns PhD, 'The Presentation of Narcissistic Personality Disorder in an Octogenarian: Converging Evidence from Multiple Sources', *Clinical Gerontologist*, Vol. 34 , no. 1, 2010, doi:10.1080/07317115.2011.524821

104 'The road to power is paved with hypocrisy' . . .: Frank Underwood, *House of Cards*, http://www.imdb.com/title/tt1856010/

104   Trump said she 'had blood coming out of her eyes . . .: Philip Rucker, 'Trump says Fox's Megyn Kelly had "blood coming out of her wherever"', *The Washington Post*, 8 August 2015, https://www.washingtonpost.com/news/post-politics/wp/2015/08/07/trump-says-foxs-megyn-kelly-had-blood-coming-out-of-her-wherever/?utm_term=.e53745290ae6

104   The closest he came to an apology . . .: Chiara Palazzo, 'Donald Trump's apology attempt to Fox host Megyn Kelly for bimbo insult – "You've been called a lot worse", *The Telegraph*, 18 May 2016.

104   'Boredom, and particularly the incredible circumstance of waking up bored . . .: Ian Fleming, *From Russia With Love*, http://www.ianfleming.com/products/from-russia-with-love/

104   Psychopaths are dopamine junkies . . .: Joshua W. Buckholtz et al., 'Mesolimbic dopamine reward system hypersensitivity in individuals with psychopathic traits', *Nature Neuroscience*, vol. 13, 2010, pp. 419–421, doi:10.1038/nn.2510

104   When we anticipate food or sex . . .: A. Nieoullon, 'Dopamine and the regulation of cognition and attention', abstract, *Progress in Neurobiology*, vol. 67, no. 1, May 2002, pp. 53–83, https://www.ncbi.nlm.nih.gov/pubmed/12126656

105   Similarly, when we are scared . . .: L. Pani et al., 'The role of stress in the pathophysiology of the dopaminergic system', abstract, *Molecular Psychiatry*, vol. 5, no. 1, January 2000, pp. 14–21, http://www.nature.com/mp/journal/v5/n1/full/4000589a.html

105   We've known for a long time that psychopathic criminals . . .: Stevens S. Smith & Joseph P. Newman, 'Alcohol and drug abuse-dependence disorders in psychopathic and nonpsychopathic criminal offenders', *Journal of Abnormal Psychology*, vol. 99, no. 4, November 1990, pp. 430–439, http://dx.doi.org/10.1037/0021-843X.99.4.430

105   And psychologists have long known that . . .: Ashley M. Hosker-Field et al., 'Psychopathy and risk taking: Examining the role of risk perception', *ScienceDirect*, vol. 91, March 2016, pp. 123–132, http://doi.org/10.1016/j.paid.2015.11.059

105   A 2010 study from Vanderbilt University . . .: Joshua W. Buckholtz.

105   Psychopaths need constant mental stimulation . . .: Herbert C. Quay, 'Psychopathic personality as pathological stimulation-seeking', *The American Journal of Psychology*, vol. 122, issue 2, August 1965, pp. 180–183, http://dx.doi.org/10.1176/ajp.122.2.180

106   A recent study performed by researchers . . .: Christina Sagioglou & Tobias Greitemeyer, 'Individual differences in bitter taste preferences are associated with antisocial personality traits', *Appetite*, vol. 96, 1 January 2016, pp. 299–308, doi.org/10.1016/j.appet.2015.09.031

106   Journalists everywhere pronounced that this meant . . .: Alex Swerdloff, 'Scientists say psychopathic people really like bitter food', *Munchies*, 10 October 2015, https://munchies.vice.com/en_us/article/scientists-say-psychopathic-people-really-like-bitter-food-58acd85b99c631c5e63ceee6

107   Our evolved ability to discriminate . . .: Lucina Q. Uddin, 'Salience processing and insular cortical function and dysfunction', *Nature Review Neuroscience* 16, 55–61 (2015), doi:10.1038/nrn3857. Published online 19 November 2014.

Chapter Three: Recognising the Everyday Psychopath (cont.)

Page

107 A 2012 Australian study . . .: M.K. Mahmut & R.J. Stevenson, 'Olfactory abilities and psychopathy: higher psychopathy scores are associated with poorer odor discrimination', *Chemosensory Perception*, vol. 5, no. 3, December 2012, pp. 300–307, doi:10.1007/s12078-012-9135-7

109 A psychopath is just as likely as an empath . . .: Steven M. Gillespie et al., 'Relations of distinct psychopathic traits with anxiety and fear: findings from offenders and non-offenders', *PlosOne*, 16 November 2015, https://doi.org/10.1371/journal.pone.0143120

109 The difference is that they do not worry about it . . .: S.S. Hoppenbrouwers et al., 'Parsing fear: a reassessment of the evidence for fear deficits in psychopathy', *Psychological Bulletin*, vol. 142, no. 6, June 2016, pp. 573–600, doi:10.1037/bul0000040

109 They live in the moment . . .: Kevin Dutton, 'Wisdom from Psychopaths?', *Scientific American Mind*, vol. 23, no. 6, January 2013, p.36, https://www.scientificamerican.com/article/wisdom-from-psychopaths/

110 Some psychopaths have reported in blogs . . .: 'Do psychopaths know they're psychopaths?', Psychopathic Writings, 21 April 2011, http.//www.psychothaic writings.com; and 'Do sociopaths know they're sociopaths?', Sociopath World, 4 December 2011, http.//www.sociopathworld.com

110 Many people have suggested that this characteristic . . .: ibid, Sociopath World.

111 'The controlling is very much an everyday occurrence . . .: C.R. Boddy, 'Psychopathic leadership: A case study of a corporate psychopath CEO', *Journal of Business Ethics*, 19 October 2015, doi:10.1007/s10551-015-2908-6

113 'Some years ago, Mr Trump invited me to lunch . . .': Richard Branson, https://www.virgin.com/richard-branson/meeting-donald-trump

114 'This particular issue came up. . .': C.R. Boddy.

115 But psychopaths are much more likely to plan and use aggression . . .: P.J. Frick et al., 'Callous-unemotional traits and conduct problems in the prediction of conduct problem severity, aggression, and self-report delinquency', *Journal of Abnormal Child Psychology*, vol. 31, no. 4, August 2003, pp. 457–470, doi:10.1023/A:1023899703866

117 Criminal psychologists have long known that psychopaths . . .: Angela Book et al., 'Psychopathy and victim selection: the use of gait as a cue to vulnerability', *Journal of Interpersonal Violence*, vol. 8, issue 11, 19 February 2013, doi:10.1177/0886260512475315

117 In 2009 researchers from Brock University . . .: S. Wheeler et al., 'Psychopathic traits and perceptions of victim vulnerability', *Criminal Justice and Behavior*, vol. 36, no. 6, 7 May 2009, pp. 635–648, doi:10.1177/0093854809333958

117 Later research by the team at Brock . . .: Angela Book et al.

120 In his study he asked 584 criminal justice and mental health workers . . .: Reid J. Meloy & M.J. Meloy, 'Autonomic arousal in the presence of psychopathy: A survey of mental health and criminal justice professionals', *Journal of Threat Assessment*, vol. 2, no. 2, 2003, pp. 21–34, http://dx.doi.org/10.1300/J177v02n02_02

Chapter Four: The Workplace Psychopath
Page

123 'Psychopaths are social predators . . .: Kate Hilpern, 'Beware: danger at work', *The Guardian*, 27 September 2004.

124 The limited studies that have been done . . .: Nathan Brooks, 'Corporate psychopaths common and can wreak havoc in business, researchers say', https:// www.psychology.org.au/news/media_releases/13September2016/Brooks/

124 He has been steadily collecting data from an online survey . . .: http://www. thegoodpsychopath.com/great-british-good-psychopath-survey/

126 Tim was bullied out of his job . . .: Will Messenger, 'Tim Field', obituary, *The Guardian*, 21 January 2006.

127 Traits of a serial bully . . .: 'Serial Bully', *Bully Online*, http://bullyonline.org/index. php/bullying/bullies/5-serial-bully

127 By 2001, Tim has formed the . . .: Hilary Freeman, 'Psycho bosses on the loose', *The Guardian*, 10 March 2001.

127 It was a view later endorsed by Robert Hare . . .: 'Serial Bully', *Bully Online*, https://bullyonline.org/index.php/bullies/5-serial-bully

127 In 2008, UK researcher Clive Boddy from Middlesex University . . .: You can see his TED talk about these studies here: https://www.youtube.com/ watch?v=tlB1pFwGhA4

128 He took a psychopathic checklist . . .: Clive R. Boddy, 'Corporate psychopaths, bullying and unfair supervision in the workplace', *Journal of Business Ethics*, vol. 100, no. 3, May 2011, pp. 367–379, doi:10.1007/s10551-010-0689-5

128 I prefer to use the term that most researchers do . . .: Richard Dembo et al., 'Levels of psychopathy and its correlates: a study of incarcerated youths in three states', *Behavioural Sciences and The Law*, vol. 25, no. 5, September/October 2007, pages 717–738, doi:10.1002/bsl.784

129 When Boddy repeated the study in UK managers . . .: Clive R. Boddy, *Corporate psychopaths: Organisational destroyers*, Palgrave Macmillan, Houndmills, Basingstoke, 2011.

Chapter Five: The Psychopath at Home
Page

135 Psychopaths know what is right and wrong . . .: Maaike Cima et al., 'Psychopaths know right from wrong but don't care', *Oxford Academic*, vol. 5, no. 1, March 2010, https://doi.org/10.1093/scan/nsp051

140 And almost all the research on psychopaths will tell you . . .: Rolf Wynn, Marita Høiseth and and Gunn Pettersen, 'Psychopathy in women: theoretical and clinical perspectives', *International Journal of Women's Health*, vol, 12, 2012, pp 257–263, doi:10.2147/IJWH.S25518

140 Little boys are much more likely than little girls . . .: Michael J. MacKenzie et al., 'Corporal punishment and child behavioural and cognitive outcomes through 5 years of age: evidence from a contemporary urban birth cohort', *Infant and Child Development*, vol. 21, no. 1, January/February 2012, pp. 3–33, doi:10.1002/icd.758

140 Researchers have found similar patterns in psychopaths . . .: Verona, E. and Vitale J. 'Psychopathy in women: assessment, manifestations and etiology', in: Patric CJ, editor. *Handbook of Psychopathy*, New York, NY: Guilford Press; 2006. pp. 415–436. See also Rolf Wynn, Marita Høiseth and and Gunn Pettersen.

Chapter Five: The Psychopath at Home (cont.)
Page

142   ...the district attorney sought maximum consecutive sentences . . .: Jim O'Hara, 'Stacey Castor gets 51 1/3 years to life imprisonment', *The Post Standard*, 5 March 2009, http://www.syracuse.com/news/index.ssf/2009/03/judge_to_sentence_murderer_sta.html

142   The judge said in his thirty-four years . . .: 'Woman sentenced in 2nd husband's poisoning', Associated Press, 5 March 2009, http://www.nbcnews.com/id/29535515/ns/us_news-crime_and_courts/t/woman-sentenced-nd-husbands-poisoning/

142   A psychiatrist interviewed by ABC television . . .: Angela Chambers & Jon Meyersohn, 'Exhumed body reveals Stacey Castor's first husband "didn't just die"', abc News, 23 April 2009, http://abcnews.go.com/2020/story?id=7394363&page=1

144   Case Study: Nigel, the psychopathic parent . . .: Nigel is a composite fictional character based on this research: https://www.researchgate.net/publication/271818253_The_Problem_of_Parental_Psychopathy

146   '[My] mother, the most beautiful person in the world . . .: Robert D. Hare, *Without conscience: The disturbing world of the psychopaths among us*, The Guilford Press, New York, 1999.

147   Case Study: Michael, the psychopathic child . . .: This is a true story reported in *The New York Times Magazine* in 2012. Jennifer Kahn, 'Can you call a 9-year-old a psychopath?', http://www.nytimes.com/2012/05/13/magazine/can-you-call-a-9-year-old-a-psychopath.html

148   Case Study: Jenny, the psychopathic neighbour . . .: Jenny is a composite fictional character based on blogs posted by people dealing with psychopathic neighbours. For example, https://www.theodysseyonline.com/10-signs-your-neighbor-psychopath; http://ajmahari.ca/2016/07/spotting-the-narcissistpsychopath-neighbor/; http://www.neighboursfromhell.com.au/The_Bitchnexdoor/sociopathy.html; http://www.psychopath-research.com/forum/ubbthreads.php/topics/14117/My_Neighbor_is_a_Psychopath; https://www.enotalone.com/forum/showthread.php?t=448274

Chapter Six: How to Manage a Workplace Psychopath
Page

153   ...there are probably more psychopaths than people with red hair . . .: Damien Gayle, 'Secret army of red heads: research reveals there are 20MILLION red hair gene carriers in the UK', *Daily Mail*, 24 August 2013, http://www.dailymail.co.uk/news/article-2401346/Ginger-genes-Research-reveals-20MILLION-red-hair-gene-carriers-Britain-Ireland.html

154   'It's better to have a hole in your team . . .: Richard Branson, 'How I Hire: Focus on Personality', *Technical Focus*, http://www.technicalfocus.com.au/how-i-hire-focus-on-personality/

156   In 2003, a newspaper gave the VK machine test . . .: Charlie Jane Anders, 'When A Newspaper Gave Blade Runner's Replicant Test To Mayor Candidates', *Gizmodo*, February 2015, http://io9.gizmodo.com/when-a-newspaper-gave-blade-runners-replicant-test-to-m-1687558534

158   In 1984, he had been fined by New York health officials . . .: Bonner, Raymond, 'Death and a doctor's past transfix Australians', *The New York Times*, 19 June 2005, http://www.nytimes.com/2005/06/19/world/asia/deaths-and-a-doctors-past-transfix-australians.html

Chapter Six: How to Manage a Workplace Psychopath (cont.)
Page

The interviewers were impressed by a glowing reference . . .: Roger Sandall, *Quadrant*, December 2005, http://www.rogersandall.com/doctor-death-in-bundaberg/

158 . . . described Patel as possessing 'technical and professional brilliance' . . .: Don Colburn & Susan Goldsmith, *The Oregonian*, 22 April 2005, 'Sanctions for doctor predate job in Oregon', http://kaiserpapers.org/formoney/patelalso bustedinny.html

158 A former US patient, John Dulley . . .: 'Patel a psychopath, says victim of surgery', *The Sydney Morning Herald*, 20 June 2005, http://www.smh.com.au/news/National/Patel-a-psychopath-says-victim-of-surgery/2005/06/19/1119119727271.html

159 The sentencing judge noted . . .: Marissa Calligeros, 'Jayant Patel finally leaves Queensland', *Brisbane Times,* 22 November 2013, http://www.brisbanetimes.com.au/queensland/jayant-patel-finally-leaves-queensland-20131122-2y0aq.html

159 'Kiss Up, Kick Down' (KUKD) manager . . .: First used to describe Robert McNamara (US Secretary of Defense under Kennedy and LBJ, during the Vietnam War) in Deborah Shapley, *Promise and power: the life and times of Robert McNamara*, Little, Brown, Boston, 1993.

159 Robert Hare and Paul Babiak described the strategies used by psychopaths . . .: Paul Babiak & Robert D. Hare, *Snakes in suits: when psychopaths go to work*, Harper Business, New York, 2006.

161 Banks rarely report the true level of credit card fraud . . .: 'Banks accused of "secrecy" after understating fraud figures', *Express*, 8 December 2014, http://www.express.co.uk/news/uk/544784/Banks-fraud-secrecy-twice-much-money-being-stolen-than-they-report

161 Recent studies have concluded . . .: P. Campanini et al., '[Workplace bullying and sickness absenteeism]', *Epidemiologia e prevenzione*, vol. 37, no. 1, Jan–Feb 2013, pp. 8–16, trans. http://www.ncbi.nlm.nih.gov/pubmed/23585429

161 They are also twice as likely . . .: A. Ortega et al, 'One-year prospective study on the effect of workplace bullying on long-term sickness absence', *Journal of Nursing Management*, vol. 19, no. 6, September 2011, pp. 752–759, doi:10.1111/j.1365-2834.2010.01179.x

162 One recent study calculated that this productivity drag . . .: A. Fattori et al., 'Estimating the impact of workplace bullying: humanistic and economic burden among workers with chronic medical conditions', *BioMed Research International*, 2015, doi:10.1155/2015/708908

162 In Australia, a study commissioned by a major health fund . . .: Medibank Private, 'The cost of workplace stress in Australia', August 2008, http://www.medibank.com.au/client/documents/pdfs/the-cost-of-workplace-stress.pdf

164 'The standard you walk past is the standard you set.' . . .: You can watch the Chief speak here: https://www.youtube.com/watch?v=QaqpoeVgr8U

164 'Ten years ago, people would have said . . .: Lynn S. Paine, 'Managing for organizational integrity', *Harvard Business Review*, March/April 1994, https://hbr.org/1994/03/managing-for-organizational-integrity Managing for Organizational Integrity

Chapter Six: How to Manage a Workplace Psychopath (cont.)
Page

165 Dishonesty in the workplace costs the average business . . .: 'The staggering cost of fraud', Association of Certified Fraud Examiners, http://www.acfe.com/rttn2016/docs/Staggering-Cost-of-Fraud-infographic.pdf

165 In 1978 Marie Bothe and Edith Gripton . . .: Al Haas, 'Company proves that honesty is best policy', *Philadelphia Inquirer*, 13 October 1991, http://articles.orlandosentinel.com/1991-10-13/business/9110110369_1_wetherill-successful-in-business-wrong-action

166 Besides absolute honesty, there were three key principles . . .: Richard W Wetherill, *Leadership into the 21st century*, The Alpha Publishing House, Royersford, Pennsylvania, 1992.

166 'Getting something for nothing . . .: ibid.

167 It has seen continuous growth since it was founded . . .: Joel Cutcher-Gershenfeld et al., 'The decline and resurgence of the U.S. auto industry', Economic Policy Institute, 6 May 2015, briefing paper #399, https://www.epi.org

169 Research consistently shows we are more likely . . .: Nina Mazar et al., 'The dishonesty of honest people: A theory of self-concept maintenance', *Journal of Marketing Research*, vol. 45, no. 6, December 2008, pp. 633–644, http://people.duke.edu/~dandan/webfiles/PapersPI/Dishonesty%20of%20Honest%20People.pdf

169 When we lie by omission . . .: M. Spranca et al., 'Omission and commission in judgment and choice', *Journal of Experimental Social Psychology*, vol. 27, 1991, pp. 76–105, https://www.sas.upenn.edu/~baron/papers.htm/oc.html

170 This insight has resulted in many tax offices worldwide . . .: 'Claiming the tax-free threshold', Australian Taxation Office, https://www.ato.gov.au/individuals/working/working-as-an-employee/claiming-the-tax-free-threshold/

170 The majority of the research in this area . . .: Lars P. Feld et al., 'Rewarding honest taxpayers? Evidence on the impact of rewards from field experiments', CREMA, http://www.webmail.crema-research.ch/papers/2006-16.pdf

171 In China, lottery numbers have been printed . . .: J. Wan, The incentive to declare taxes and tax revenue: the lottery receipt experiment in China, paper prepared for the 64th Congress of the International Institute of Public Finance, University of Maastricht, The Netherlands, 2008.

171 In the UK, customers who pay their council tax . . .: 'Applying behavioural insights to reduce fraud, error and debt', Cabinet Office Behavioural Insights Team, 2012, https://www.gov.uk/government/uploads/system/uploads/attachment_data/file/60539/BIT_FraudErrorDebt_accessible.pdf

176 Follett recognised the role of 'soft' factors . . .: Mary P. Follett, 'The giving of orders', *Scientific foundations of business administration*, H.C. Metcalf & H.A. Overstreet, Williams & Wilkins, Baltimore, 1926, pp. 29–37.

177 The HP Way . . .: http://www.hpalumni.org/hp_way

179 This, for example, is Intel's 2013 Corporate Mission Statement . . .: https://www.strategicmanagementinsight.com/mission-statements/intel-mission-statement.html

181 What now emerges I think . . .: C.R. Boddy, 'Psychopathic leadership: A case study of a corporate psychopath CEO', *Journal of Business Ethics*, 19 October 2015, doi:10.1007/s10551-015-2908-6

Chapter Six: How to Manage a Workplace Psychopath (cont.)
Page
185 A 2016 study of Australian workplaces . . .: V. Webster, et al., 'Fight, flight or freeze:
common responses for follower coping with toxic leadership', *Stress & Health*,
vol. 32, no. 4, October 2016, pp. 346–354, doi:10.1002/smi.2626
188 Renowned expert on English Linguistics . . .: Leech, G.N., *Principles of pragmatics*,
Longman, New York, 1983.

Chapter Seven: Dealing with Psychopaths in Your Personal Life
Page
200 Obviously if psychopaths are as prevalent . . .: C.S. Neumann, 'Will the real
psychopath please stand up?', University of North Texas, https://research.unt.edu/
research-profiles/will-real-psychopath-please-stand
202 The research clearly demonstrates that parenting style does not affect . . .:
M. Oxford et al., 'Callous/unemotional traits moderate the relation between ineffective
parenting and child externalizing problems: a partial replication and extension',
Journal of Clinical Child & Adolescent Psychology, vol. 32, no. 4, 2003, doi:10.1207/
S15374424JCCP3204_10; and Mark R. Dadds et al., 'Love, eye contact and the
developmental origins of empathy v. psychopathy', *The British Journal of Psychiatry*,
vol. 200, no. 3, March 2012, pp. 191–196, doi:10.1192/bjp.bp.110.085720

Chapter Eight: What Does All this Mean for Society?
Page
211 We are one of the very few animals that hunt . . .: Richard D. Alexander, 'The
evolution of social behavior', Museum of Zoology and Department of Zoology,
University of Michigan, Ann Arbor, Michigan 48104, http://courses.washington.
edu/ccab/Alexander1974.pdf
211 Without it, we would simply compete with other unrelated humans . . .: Charles
Stangor, *Principles of Social Psychology*, BC Open Textbooks, https://opentextbc.ca/
socialpsychology/chapter/conflict-cooperation-morality-and-fairness/
211 A landmark study . . .: S.L.A. Marshall, *Men against fire: The problem of battle
command*, University of Oklahoma Press, 2000, p.54.
211 Killing in combat for a psychologically normal individual . . .: Stephen Evans, 'How
soldiers deal with the job of killing', BBC News, 11 June 2011, http://www.bbc.
com/news/world-13687796
212 In humans, researchers have proposed . . .: J. Moll, et al., 'The neural correlates of
moral sensitivity: a functional magnetic resonance imaging investigation of basic
and moral emotions', *The Journal of Neuroscience*, vol. 22, no. 7, 1 April 2002,
pp. 2730–2736, http://www.jneurosci.org/content/22/7/2730.full.pdf
212 Studies have definitively established that . . .: Robert Thornberg, 'A study of
children's conceptions of school rules by investigating their judgements of
transgressions in the absence of rules', *Educational Psychology*, vol. 30, no. 5, 2010,
pp. 583–603, doi:10.1080/01443410.2010.492348
213 Case study: Ava the intelligent machine . . .: Based on Tim Urban's lengthy and brilliant
description of super intelligent machine learning, 'The AI revolution: our immortality
or extinction', http://waitbutwhy.com/2015/01/artificial-intelligence-revolution-2.html.
The name Ava comes from the movie *Ex Machina*, about the first AI machine.

Chapter Eight: What Does All this Mean for Society? (cont.)

Page

217 'On our little island of human psychology . . .: ibid.

217 Psychopaths do not distinguish between moral and social rules . . .: R.J. Blair, 'A cognitive developmental approach to morality: investigating the psychopath', *Cognition*, vol. 57, no. 1, October 1995, pp. 1–29, http://www.ncbi.nlm.nih.gov/pubmed/7587017

220 Professor Dan Ariely from Duke University . . .: Dan Ariely, *The honest truth about dishonesty: How we lie to everyone – especially ourselves*, Harper Collins, London, 2012.

223 In 2011, researchers from the Harvard Business School . . .: Lisa L. Shu, 'Signing at the beginning makes ethics salient and decreases dishonest self-reports in comparison to signing at the end', Proceedings of the National Academy of Sciences of the United States of America, vol. 109, no. 38, pp. 15197–15200, doi:10.1073/pnas.1209746109

Chapter Nine: How Culture Creates Psychopaths

Page

225 Psychology literature from the last century . . .: R.D. Hare, 'The Hare PCL-R: some issues concerning its use and misuse', *Legal and Criminological Psychology*, vol. 3, no. 1, February 1998, pp. 99–119, doi:10.1111/j.2044-8333.1998.tb00353.x

225 One study compared the US with Taiwan . . .: W.M. Compton et al., 'New methods in cross-cultural psychiatry: psychiatric illness in Taiwan and the United States', *American Journal of Psychiatry*, vol. 148, no. 12, December 1991, pp. 1697–1704, doi:10.1176/ajp.148.12.1697

226 Sociologists call societies that favour tight-knit community groups . . .: J.W. Berry et al., *Cross-cultural psychology: Research and applications*, Cambridge University Press, 1992.

226 Collective cultures encourage subservience . . .: ibid; and D. Leake & R. Black, *Essential tools – Cultural and linguistic diversity: Implications for transition personal*, Minneapolis, University of Minnesota, Institute on Community Integration, National Center on Secondary Education and Transition, 2005.

227 Around 85% of world fish stocks are now over-exploited . . .: Vince Gaia, 'How the world's oceans could be running out of fish', BBC, 21 September 2012, http://www.bbc.com/future/story/20120920-are-we-running-out-of-fish

227 The study has since been continuously updated . . .: Geert Hofstede et al., *Cultures and organizations: Software of the mind*, 3rd edn, McGraw-Hill, New York, 2010.

228 It's probably no coincidence that as Australia progressed . . .: 'The Incidence of Accepted Workers' Compensation Claims for Mental Stress in Australia', Safe Work Australia, April 2013, https://safeworkaustralia.gov.au/system/files/documents/1702/the-incidence-accepted-wc-claims-mental-stress-australia.pdf

231 In the 1880s almost one in three boys . . .: Popular baby names by decade, Social Security Administration, https://www.ssa.gov/oact/babynames/decades/index.html

233 It might seem like social media platforms . . .: D. Chaffey, 'Global social media research summary', 27 February 2017, http://www.smartinsights.com/social-media-marketing/social-media-strategy/new-global-social-media-research/

Chapter Nine: How Culture Creates Psychopaths (cont.)

Page

236 The research clearly shows that collectivist societies . . .: R.D. Hare, 'Psychopathy, affect and behaviour', *Psychopathy: theory, research, and implications for society*, eds D. Cooke, A. Forth & R. Hare, Dordrecht, Kluwer, 1998, pp. 105–139.

237 'In an unregulated world . . .: 'Brian Basham: Beware corporate psychopaths – they are still occupying positions of power', *Independent*, 29 December 2011, http://www.independent.co.uk/news/business/comment/brian-basham-beware-corporate-psychopaths-they-are-still-occupying-positions-of-power-6282502.html

240 Since 2000 the world's largest ad agency . . .: 2017 Edelman Trust Barometer, http://www.edelman.com/global-results/

ACKNOWLEDGEMENTS

Many people who don't want to be named or identified in any way whatsoever need to be acknowledged for the book you have just read. It is a trademark of the psychopath that they frequently ruin lives so thoroughly and are so likely to seek revenge for any slight, be it real or perceived, that even people who have not seen them for decades still crave anonymity. To all the people who shared their stories, thank you.

My wife, Lizzie, has as always been my thought-editor in chief. She is the sanity checker, the notion challenger and the logic tester. She had also spent many an hour without the (dubious) benefit of my company so this book could be written. And she has made sure the arguments it makes stand up to the close examination I hope every reader will bring to bear upon it. Without Lizzie this book would be nothing but a twinkle in my eye.

I have been wanting to write this book for a very long time and my publisher, Ingrid Ohlsson, has been wanting to publish it for almost as long. But we both had to complete my jottings on food before we could start. Taking this from a rough idea to the book you hold in your hands has in no small part been made possible by Ingrid's certainty that this book on this topic needed to be written by me.

As my editor at Pan Macmillan, Georgia Douglas had the thankless task of making sure we hit all the editing deadlines and nagging me to death until we did. Her fastidious attention to detail has ensured the whole project actually happened and more than that, was as precisely formed as my writing could ever be.

I have a tendency to write things in the order I discover them. This rarely makes for a coherent narrative. Without Ariane Durkin, the structural editor, the sleek narrative you've just read would be significantly more difficult to follow. She uncovered the themes I had spread about the place and dragged them together in a coherent stream of argument. Of course, it was exactly what I'd been thinking all along. No, really.

I'm not even sure my agent, Frank Stranges, knows I've written this book. Ah, the life of an agent, just sit back and wait for the cheques.

And finally, I want to thank all those publishers and authors who happily gave me permission to quote from their books and their papers without demanding any form of payment or compensation. That attitude helps all of our ideas propagate more widely and I am very grateful.

MORE FROM DAVID GILLESPIE
FREE SCHOOLS

Bestselling author David Gillespie shows parents how to choose the best school for their kids, how to avoid fees, and how to make a less-than-perfect system better.

David Gillespie has six kids. Like many parents, he and his wife faced some tough decisions when it came to choosing a high school. He calculated that sending his kids to a private school would cost him $1.3 million. A businessman at heart, he thought it worth doing some research to find out what he'd get for his money. In other words, would his kids get better results? The answer was no.

Intrigued, David continued his research, only to discover he was wrong on most counts – as are most parents – when it comes to working out what factors deliver a great education. Among other things, he found out that class size doesn't matter, composite classes are fine, fancy buildings and rolling lawns are a waste of money, the old-school-tie network won't cut it in the new industries and NAPLAN is misread by everyone so is largely meaningless as a measure of quality.

Taking on an entrenched system of vested interests – the unions, the government, our own sense of worth, privilege and entitlement – this book is both a practical guide to getting the best for our kids and a provocative overview of why the system is struggling.

EAT REAL FOOD

The only solution to permanent weight loss and disease prevention.

In the last 100 years, we've become fatter and sicker, with millions of people developing serious diseases from diabetes to cancer. Health gurus confuse us with complex diets, expensive 'superfoods' and conflicting advice, while food manufacturers load their products with addictive and destructive ingredients causing our increasing weight and declining health. But help is at hand. Health and consumer advocate David Gillespie, a man who shed forty kilos and kept it off, shares the simple secret of weight loss and wellbeing: swap processed food for REAL FOOD.

Eat Real Food features:

- An explanation of why diets don't work and a focus on what does.
- Information on how to lose weight permanently, not just in the short-term.
- Evidence-based science explaining the real culprits of ill health and weight gain.
- Advice on how to read food labels.
- Easy recipes to replace common processed items and meal plans that show how simple it is to shop, plan and cook Real Food.
- Tips for lunchboxes, parties, and recipes for food kids actually like.

Eat Real Food is the safe, effective and cheap – AND ONLY – solution to losing weight and improving our health permanently.

THE EAT REAL FOOD COOKBOOK

For nearly ten years, David Gillespie has warned us of the dangers of sugar, and Australia has listened. More recently he has alerted us to the other toxin in our food supply: seed oil. Most processed food – from French fries to yoghurt to spreadable butter – contains one or both of these ingredients, so the question is: how do we eat real food?

Expanding on his 2015 bestseller *Eat Real Food*, David shows us how to:

- Identify and avoid sugar- and seed-oil-laden supermarket products
- Identify and shop for the healthy options
- Make the foods we normally buy in jars and packets – from mayonnaise to bread to tomato sauce
- Make simple, inexpensive daily meals the entire family will love
- Pack and plan for meals away from home
- Create healthier treats for all occasions, from kids' birthdays to cocktail parties

The Eat Real Food Cookbook is your guide to saying 'no' to the food that manufacturers want you to eat and 'yes' to the sort of food that will help you manage your weight and the long-term health of your family.